Two-Year-Olds in Early Years Settings

Two-Year-Olds in Early Years Settings

Journeys of Discovery

Julia Manning-Morton and Maggie Thorp

Open University Press

Open University Press
McGraw-Hill Education
McGraw-Hill House
Shoppenhangers Road
Maidenhead
Berkshire
England
SL6 2QL

email: enquiries@openup.co.uk
world wide web: www.openup.co.uk

and Two Penn Plaza, New York, NY 10121-2289, USA

First published 2015

A catalogue record of this book is available from the British Library

ISBN–13: 978-0-33-526402-5 (pb)
ISBN–10: 0-33-526402-6 (pb)
eISBN: 978-0-33-526403-2

Library of Congress Cataloging-in-Publication Data
CIP data applied for

Typesetting and e-book compilations by
RefineCatch Limited, Bungay, Suffolk

Praise for this book

This is a book after my own heart because the authors really understand two year olds and what they need in order to flourish. The case studies are carefully chosen to illuminate what it is to be two years old. It is beautifully written , so that both heart and mind of the reader are engaged. The book equips practitioners and managers to be informed about the development and learning and cultural context of this, so that they can enjoy spending time and finding the energy and confidence needed for work with and for two year olds. I could not put this book down.

Professor Tina Bruce CBE, Froebel Trust

At a time of considerable political interest this book presents a timely focus on the uniqueness of working with 2-year-olds and their families. A strength of this book is the thoughtful use of case studies interwoven throughout each chapter – the authors use these to encourage the reader to make deeper connections with the theoretical perspectives that underpin their practice. The encouragement of readers to thoughtfully reflect on their practice will undoubtedly support practitioners in delivering appropriate high quality care and education for 2-year-olds and thus support them on their journeys and discoveries. A thorough exploration of the developmental paths of 2-year-olds coupled with the importance of individual children's socio-cultural contexts enables readers to gain a true understanding of the characteristics of 2-year-olds. An essential text for practitioners, leaders and students on Early Childhood Studies degrees and Early Years Initial Teacher Training (EYITT) programmes.

*Kelly Cooper, Programme Director for EYITT
– London Metropolitan University*

No matter what your starting point, you could not read this book without gaining greater understanding and respect for young children. Talk of peaceful caregiving, joyful play, abundant language, companionship and partnership permeate the pages leaving the reader with a profound sense of awe for the enormity of the task facing both two year olds in their quest to find themselves and their carers in supporting them through that process. The book is practical – each chapter offers case studies and reflection points and provides short outlines of key theoretical ideas. But most of all I loved the emphasis on ample space and the need for children and carers to take time - without rush, and with warmth, gentleness and respect.

Linda Pound, Freelance Early Years Consultant

This is an important and timely book, providing a wonderful resource for all who are striving to develop their practice and provision for two year olds. The authors , informed by the 'real life' complexities faced by practitioners in schools and settings, effortlessly blend research and theory and invite all of us working alongside two year olds to examine our own theories of practice. This journey of discovery becomes not only about deepening our understanding of the unique and particular characteristics of two year olds, but is turned inwards, encouraging us to become self-aware and more able to adopt a critical stance and challenge common assumptions about everyday practice.
Janice Darkes-Sutcliffe (School Improvement Liverpool)

Contents

Introduction

When writing about young children's development and learning, the analogy of a 'journey' is, perhaps at first glance, an easy one to make. After all, don't children 'travel' along a developmental route? Yes they do, but this book aims not only to describe aspects of the route travelled by 2-year-olds but also to explore some problematic ideas about that route. We want to highlight the particular position 2-year-olds are in – they are not babies but nor are they 3- and 4-year-olds; calling them 'rising 3s' as we have sometimes heard said at conferences, does not take away their 'twoness'. As might be expected, in this book we emphasize that each child follows their own pathways as well as sharing roads with others. Each child's journey and the routes they take will reflect their individual interests, concerns and character traits. We also assert that those paths are not linear, going from A to B, but that they wind, loop, pause and double back, as well as stretch out ahead. Our experience as practitioners, researchers and advisors in early years settings has shown us that when this is understood and appreciated, those working with 2-year-olds will provide wonderful lands to discover and explore and offer just the right level of support to enable children to do so.

A key aim of this book is to help all the adults responsible for provision for this age group to reflect on and understand better what it is like to be 2 years old and therefore what the implications are for policy and practice in early years settings. We think this understanding comes from three things:

- a thorough knowledge of child development and how young children learn;
- an understanding of each individual child and their socio-cultural contexts;
- time and support to reflect both on personal experience and on provision for 2-year-olds.

As regards the first of these, we do not mean merely knowing developmental 'norms'; rather, we believe it is important to understand how particular aspects of 2-year-olds' development combine to generate common characteristics and how these common characteristics blend with children's individual temperaments and dispositions as a result of the constant interaction between the child's biological endowment and their socio-cultural context. For example, some people like to go on holiday to the same place each year. They feel secure in knowing the area well, repeating familiar experiences and enjoying the continuity of the relationships they have made with local people. Others prefer the variety of visiting different places, the challenge of finding their way around a new area and the stimulation of trying something new such as a food or a language. Some 2-year-olds' temperaments or dispositions may mean they generally tend to be more one sort of traveller or the other. However, most 2-year-olds are a combination of these two kinds of traveller and their common characteristic of emotional and behavioural changeability means that they can veer between wanting the more predictable path and craving the adventure of the unknown territory very quickly. These aspects of 2-year-olds' development are considered in Chapter 1 of this book.

Chapter 1 also focuses on the centrality of 2-year-olds' home lives. The current policy focus on 2-year-olds in England (Mathers et al. 2009) emphasizes the importance of early learning but by so doing also infers that the best place for that to happen is in early childcare and education settings. This attitude could lead practitioners to forget or not realize the wide range of everyday life experiences that most children participate in with their close adults at home and in their communities. These are experiences from which they learn huge amounts and which neuroscientists such as Gopnik et al. (1999) say can be the kind of positive experiences that are most useful for early brain development. The importance we ascribe to this idea means that it is the focus of the first chapter in the book; for only by creating strong links with those home experiences and developing equally rich, varied and relevant experiences in and beyond the setting will practitioners truly enrich 2-year-olds' lives.

This book is not only about the developmental journeys of 2-year-olds; it is also about the journey that many 2-year-olds are setting out on as they go from their home to the childcare and education setting and back again each day. This is a major venture, the success of which will be shaped by the bridges that are built between these two landscapes and how parent and practitioner guides smooth the path of the 2-year-old as they cross the bridge. As their world widens, 2-year-olds are constantly meeting new, challenging and often hard to understand experiences. One of these is starting in an early years setting and separating from their parents for prolonged periods, perhaps for the first time. If one considers how, even as adults, being in new situations can be really daunting, one can appreciate that such big changes in a 2-year-old's life will inevitably lead to mood and behaviour swings. Therefore in Chapter 2 we focus on settling-in processes and how this sets the tone for the child's and family's future relationships with the setting. We explore what joining a new group means for 2-year-olds and what the Key Person and the setting manager need to consider to ensure this process is focused on the child's and the family's needs.

It is our contention that a 2-year-old's enjoyment of their journey in an early years setting and how much they learn on the way is strongly influenced by *all* their experiences, so attention must be paid to the whole curriculum. Hence, woven into each chapter of the book, there is discussion on how the setting's unplanned psychological structure of relationships, routines and environment is organized. This hidden curriculum often implicitly conveys the values and beliefs of the practitioners, which influence practitioners' ideas and perspectives on the child's journey. Practitioners may believe that there is a particular destination that they want children to reach so there is a specific route they need to follow or they might think that their role is just to follow along behind and see where children end up. The degree to which children take the lead in their journey or are guided by adults is a fundamental pedagogical question that practitioners, whether working alone or in teams, need to be clear about. The level and type of support the 2-year-old needs and how the role of Key Person can provide this are the focus of Chapter 3. It explores ways in which the Key Person can shape the settings' daily routines to better meet 2-year-olds' needs and concerns.

They say that every journey starts with a single step, meaning that to get where you want to go in life, you have to take a first action or decision, indicating that the first step is therefore a momentous one. However, other elements such as confidence or resolve will need to be in place before that first step is taken and there are important subsequent events too. In every journey there are decisions about how to travel, directions to go in and whether or where to settle, all influenced by the people you meet along the way. Similarly, babies' first steps and first words, for example, are seen as significant but so are the previous crawling and babbling. And of course, the subsequent skills of hopping, jumping and talking in sentences will be refined according to the hurdles or easy rides of the child's experience and the people around them, who play a substantial part in influencing a child's route map. Our perspective here then, is that as development is a continuum, it is necessary always to understand what went before and what may come after, as in any group of 2-year-olds each child will be different to the others in maturity as they travel along different pathways at different rates. Individual children will be at different stages in particular aspects of development, more mature physically and less mature socially, for example, as one aspect of development seems to remain static while the child seems to be focussing on another, or while events in their lives take up their energies.

So the third year of life is a significant period of consolidation of the huge amount of learning and development that has gone on in a child's first two years, but it also involves many, varied and rapid developmental changes. One of these is the ability to communicate verbally, which usually takes a significant leap forward in the third year. This is explored in Chapter 5 where particular attention is paid to the idiosyncrasies of 2-year-olds' talk and where we discuss the importance of adults knowing the child and the context really well in order to have meaningful conversations with them. The interesting journey of children learning more than one language is also explored.

The 2-year-old's growing ability to communicate enables friendships to grow. In Chapter 4 some of the myths about 2-year-olds' ability to make and sustain friendships are challenged and the value of friendships and ways in which practitioners can recognize and support them are investigated. Entering an early years setting also brings children into contact with adults and children whose ways, appearance and language differ from their own. Two-year-olds' interest and curiosity about diversity are also a focal point of this chapter, with discussion on how positive dispositions to difference can be fostered to promote children's understanding of self and others.

At this age, children's emotional regulation is making huge strides and their language and social skills are rapidly growing yet all these skills are still relatively immature. The 'unpredictable-ness' and 'out of their control-ness' of life can result in mood swings and switches between fierce independence and a desire to be held. By this age the 2-year-old will have learnt much about adult expectations of how to behave but may really struggle to consistently co-operate with these demands. In Chapter 6 we explore in some detail why this is so. We describe a partnership approach that can help the 2-year-old retain a positive sense of self as they struggle with the frustrations of being part of a group and meeting the different expectations of adults in the setting and at home.

A common characteristic of 2-year-olds is their love of being active, on the go and into everything, activity that enables them to refine the phenomenal physical skills gained in the first two years. So providing for both safety and independence and the value of risk-taking are discussed in Chapter 7. At this age, a child's birth experience, such as being premature, as well as their early home experiences will influence their individual development hugely. A child who is nearly 3 is, therefore, very different to when they were just 2 and what exactly that is like will be different for each child and some children will have additional and specific needs that have to be addressed. In this respect, Chapter 7 discusses how to consider the concerns of parents, practitioners and managers in relation to physical learning and risk but still provide for children's well-being.

Being 2 seems like a jumping off point in many ways: jumping from their secure base of home into the wider world, jumping off from concrete sensory learning into the world of imagination and symbols, leaping into language, and diving into vast pools of knowledge, and, underpinning it all, literally jumping (and running and climbing and crawling). But where will this child land? This is a journey with an unknown destination, so what is important is that each moment is enjoyed as much as possible; that the landscape the child is in *now* is contemplated at leisure, rather than rushed through like a train en route to 'school readiness' terminus, stopping only at literacy central and numeracy junction! In Chapter 8 we explore how 2-year-olds' growing knowledge and understanding can be understood and fostered. A key idea in this regard is 'reciprocal interweaving' (Gesell 1952, cited in Piek 2006), which suggests that in addition to socio-cultural influences, there is also a biological influence on the more overarching changes we can observe over the third year of life, physically, cognitively and socially. This idea is based on Gesell's maturational theory and discusses the relationship between the growth of structures in the brain or the body and a person's behaviours. This perspective suggests that development moves in a progressive spiral, through a process in which there are stages of equilibrium, when things are comfortably balanced between two possible poles and stages of disequilibrium, when things are out of kilter and lean towards one pole or the other. The process of equilibrium being lost is repeated until a more advanced form of behaviour emerges. This perspective is usually used to look at physical developments such as the development of binocular vision or handedness but may also consider personality development such as moving between being shy and outgoing, compliant or defiant. It is a perspective that can help us to understand that 2-year-olds are not all 'terrible' all the time but will move through periods of balance and instability at different times throughout the third year of life (and beyond).

Practitioners who understand the winding developmental paths of 2-year-olds are more able to develop an 'abundance' (Thorp 2003) model of provision, focussing on what 2-year-olds have an abundance of and enjoy rather than what they lack. Therefore, in Chapter 9 we emphasize the relevance of the underpinning principle of the 'Unique Child' in the Early Years Foundation Stage guidance (DFE 2014a) and the key role of observation when planning for individual 2-year-olds. This chapter also stresses how practitioners need to adopt a flexible approach when organizing their group, expecting differences between children and avoiding practices that pressurize 2-year-olds into doing the same thing at the same time, such as learning to use the toilet, thread beads or give up their feeder cup or bottle. Our aim is to encourage practitioners to be reflective, so that, as the children in their group changes, they are able to plan and discuss how to alter their expectations of children and adapt the play environment, play opportunities and care routines according to their observations of that particular group of children.

Where a child lands when they jump off into the wider world, whether they land on their feet or fall on their faces (or belly flop), depends hugely on the adults around them. It depends on whether the adults push them before they are ready or hold them back or whether they hold their hand or are there ready to catch them, should they need it.

All this requires that practitioners working with 2-year-olds need to have a good understanding of themselves as well as of the children. So in Chapter 10 we explore the necessary skills, attributes and support needs of practitioners. We suggest that an essential attribute is being interested in working alongside 2-year-olds, rather than having power over them, but acknowledge that the challenges of working with the intense and fluctuating needs of this age group also influence one's own feelings and values. Many practitioners are motivated by a desire to make things 'better' for children and families but are then working in situations or with families that make this extremely difficult. Therefore, practitioners need frequent and regular opportunities to reflect on their practice and to see where they are 'good enough' as Winnicott says (1957). To be clear, this does not mean a low baseline of mediocre practice, it means thinking about how can we be good enough for this child to feel good about themselves/to want to explore and find out about the world/to have a sense of belonging/to fly?

For many of us working with, studying and writing about very young children, much of the above (and possibly what follows!) is not new. So it would be reasonable to ask why this (and other) books on 2-year-olds are being written at this time. The answer lies of course in the current political interest in the early years in general and most recently in England, in 2-year-olds in particular.

The UK government introduced its policy on free childcare places for eligible 2-year-olds in 2006 and since then has invested millions of pounds in the sector to create a total of 260,000 places (DFE 2013a). This considerable investment has happened despite the intense pressure on public spending at the current time, so must represent a strong political idea. We believe that this idea is based on arguments of future economic benefit rather than a commitment to high quality provision which supports all children and families. It derives in part from a series of American studies conducted since the 1960s which suggested that 'investing 1 dollar in early childhood brings a return of 7 dollars when the children grow up, mainly because they are less likely to commit crimes or other misdemeanours' (Penn 2008: 155). These studies provide the economic arguments in support of policies about young children's care and education focusing on early intervention for 'vulnerable' or 'disadvantaged' 2-year-olds.

This has resulted in funding for childcare places (of 15 hours a week) for 2-year olds but only for what the UK government report as: 'around 92,000 of the most disadvantaged 2-year-olds' (DFE 2013a). In this way this policy perpetuates the historical tradition in the UK, whereby young children have been viewed as the private responsibility of the family rather than a public responsibility, unless there is a perceived difficulty. This has meant that historically the UK government – in comparison to Scandinavian countries for example – has invested less in the early years sector, leaving the majority of provision in the hands of private business. Despite a decade of intensive reform and total spending of £17 billion from 1997 to 2006 on services for young children, parents in Britain still pay 70 per cent of their childcare costs compared to the European average of 30 per cent (Hakim et al. 2008). In addition, while there has been a substantial increase in investment in the early years in the UK since the late 1990s, it has been primarily focussed on 'education' for over 3-year-olds rather than full-day care as in the Nordic countries. So the idea that the state only gets involved when children are in need or disadvantaged lingers on.

Our concern is that this results in a stigmatized, 'one-size-fits-all' approach to providing for children and families. Many 2-year-olds, whilst disadvantaged economically, have warm, caring home lives and so find separation manageable and the policy may help their parents to find part-time work to ease the family's financial situation. However, other 2-year-olds, who have experienced disrupted relationships with attachment figures, or whose parents are finding parenting a challenge, are not necessarily best helped by going to a day care setting, especially if that setting is not well resourced for giving skilled support and advice work, or providing secure, warm and consistent care through an effective Key Person relationship. Poor physical environments or poor diet and health and social stigma are all factors which have a profound effect on young children's mental health and resilience as identified by The Well-Being Project (Manning-Morton 2014) and The Millennium Cohort Study (Sabates and Dex 2012). So some settings are not only having to adjust to and learn about the particular characteristics common to 2-year-olds but also to working with 2-year-olds and their families who may have additional complex factors in their lives.

We are also concerned that the speed of implementation of this policy and the resulting arrangements local authorities and providers are making are compromising practitioners' efforts at developing high quality provision. As the Government's own evaluation of the pilot scheme showed (DFE 2013b), it is only high quality settings that make a positive difference to children's lives but the speed of expansion is resulting in no time for local authorities to support settings in developing their services. In addition, the pressure to offer many new places is resulting in providers structuring provision to address economies of scale rather than the needs of the children. To meet targets and to gain from the funding attached to 2-year-olds, settings are creating large groups of 2-year-olds or are incorporating them into large groups of 3- to 5-year-olds. Practitioners report that their settings are arranging for 2-year-olds to attend in shifts, thereby enabling three different groups of 2-year-olds to attend for three-hour funded sessions. The impact of such an arrangement is that practitioners are trying to build relationships with, hold in mind, and meet the individual needs of three times as many children and families! Inevitably in these kinds of situations, there is a risk that the quality of provision for many vulnerable 2-year-olds will be low or mediocre. This is then a double dose of disadvantage.

The impact of how part-time places for 2-year-olds are arranged also gives rise to concern. Often, arrangements of part-time places result in the membership of groups changing on a daily basis. This does not provide the kind of cohesive relational environment that supports emotional and social well-being and builds resilience in very young children. Integrating 2-year-olds into large groups of 3–5-year-olds can also adversely affect this. Mixing the UK statutory ratio of one adult to four 2-year-olds with the 1:8 ratio for over 3-year-olds (DFE 2014a) can result in one Key Person trying to meet the needs of six children: two of whom are 2 years old and four 3 to 5 years old. This can lead to the particular needs of the younger children (who, in the funded scheme, may also have additional needs) being overlooked, resulting in behaviours that bring distress to the whole group such as emotional collapses and hitting out or withdrawing.

It is in this context that we write this book on supporting 2-year-olds in early years settings. We aim to share some of our knowledge and understanding and offer practitioners, practice leaders, students on early years degrees and managers of settings a theoretical underpinning of 2-year-old's development and learning, which they can use to argue for good practice and resist inappropriate top-down or external pressure from senior managers or regulatory bodies. Much of the theory and practice included in this book is discussed on the courses we have developed and run both in higher education and as Inset professional development 'Key Times' courses, where practitioners also share their practice wisdom and dilemmas with us. So, interwoven through each chapter are many practical examples of how young children can experience high quality care and education and ways in which practitioners can reflect on their own life experiences to determine what is best for the 2-year-olds in their care. We hope you find it useful!

1 Home is where I start from

Introduction

No one can deny that we are all products of our families, yet we are also who we are as a result of many other influences. Each 2-year-old is a unique individual so practitioners need to keep in mind that in any group of 2-year-olds each child will be different to the others in personality. Two-year-old children will have already developed quite distinct styles in their approach to life, learning and other people. Some will be gregarious and chatty, others reserved and shy; some will be lively and adventurous, others placid or cautious. In this chapter we will explore different perspectives on how these characteristics develop.

Two-year-olds will also have already absorbed a huge amount of under-standing within their families about what is expected of them according to their family position and culture. Some will be expected to feed themselves with implements, others not. Some will be used to the rough and tumble of being in a group of other children, others will find such a situation new and overwhelming. In this way, a 2-year-old's personality development is hugely influenced by the social group of their family and later in this chapter we will consider the fundamental importance of positive attachment relationships and the impact of different parenting styles on young children's sense of self.

How the family group influences the child is in turn influenced by their socio-economic and cultural context; young children's well-being is affected by the well-being of their close adults. But as well as issues such as poverty, discrimination and social inequality impacting on 2-year-olds' well-being (Dickins 2014), the positive or negative attitudes and responses of others to a 2-year-old's family and home context are also a major factor that influences their sense of self and self-esteem. This chapter therefore discusses the importance of practitioners reflecting on their values and beliefs about families as an essential ingredient of developing a positive approach to working in partnership with parents.

Case studies

Tola (2y6m) is an only child living with his mother, Adetutu; his father died when Tola was 6 months old. They are from Nigeria and are Christians and although they have very little family in the UK, Tola and his mother see their church as their extended family; Tola calls the adults 'auntie' and 'uncle' and he loves playing with the 'big boys'. Adetutu has been waiting a year and nine months for indefinite leave to stay in the UK from the Home Office and they live in emergency accommodation – one room with shared kitchen and bathroom. She does care work on a zero hours contract so her income is low and unpredictable. Tola is tall for his age and looks 3 or 4 years old. He is lively and curious: 'into everything, afraid of nothing', his mother says. She worries about him getting sick or hurt. She says, 'Everything I've been through will be worth it to see Tola grow up safe, healthy, and doing well.' When asked about her aspirations for Tola she says: "I want him to learn, to do really well, get into good schools, to university.' Adetutu sees this as Tola's ticket out of poverty and low status; she loves Tola asking questions and tries to give good explanations. She worries about Tola wanting birthday parties or wanting to invite his nursery friends to play at his home because of their circumstances.

* * *

Aisling (2y5m) is the third and youngest child in her family. Her brothers are 6 and 8. Her parents are both Irish and are teachers, working full-time. Aisling's father says she is very talkative, always asking questions, but mainly when with the family. He describes her as 'rather shy when with others, unlike her brothers'. Aisling's parents love the outdoors, they cycle to work and Aisling rides on her parents' bikes to the nursery. They go for walks at weekends and camping in the summer. When asked about their hopes and concerns for Aisling as she grows up, her mother says: 'Aisling is already very concerned about others, stroking her brothers if they get upset and she loves to help. I hope that she'll make good friends throughout life and continue to be caring – not get cynical. She loves animals, even spiders. We want her to take on our concern for the environment.' Her father said: 'I hope she grows out of being so shy, I sometimes feel impatient with her for not enjoying company, especially as we are always having friends and family to stay. She just seems to retreat into herself, not crying, just really quiet. We Skype my mother, who thinks she can't talk – if only they could hear her when she's just with us!'

Personality development

Personality development is a central focus for 2-year-olds; as Anne Stonehouse says (1990: 3), 2-year-olds are 'person creating', exploring their own and others' ideas of who they are. Their conclusions are arrived at through a complex process that combines the biological influences of temperament and physical attributes with the socio-cultural influences of relationships within their family, community and wider society. This reflects an interactionist perspective on development; that development is a constant interaction between the biological self and social experience (Schaffer 2006).

Biology affects personality in a range of ways. First, the sex, ethnicity and/or disability of a child will influence how others treat them and how they expect the child to behave. For example, parents/carers have different expectations of boy babies and girl babies from birth (Stern et al. 1995) and handle them differently, with boys being handled more vigorously, such as bouncing and holding up in the air, while girls are held closely and smiled at more (Stern and Karraker 1989). In this way 2-year-olds will have already been developing an understanding of themselves as part of a particular social category and in this process, will have received social 'scripts' (Berne 1970) about how a child in this particular category is expected to be. The degree to which these expectations match the child's inner self-image will impact on their self-esteem. So, for example, a boy who does not enjoy vigorous physical activity may feel lacking in some way because he does not meet others' stereotyped expectations of boys being boisterous. For 2-year-olds, it is the physical manifestations of self that are the most meaningful and easily understood, rooted as they are in their bodies and physical experience, so the responses of others to their physical 'selves' has a direct impact on their emotional and personality development. For example, Tola's physical size means he is expected to behave like a 4-year-old by those who don't know his age.

Another way in which adults' interactions with 2-year-olds impact on their sense of self is through the parents' or practitioners' response to the child's temperament. Some temperament types fit into some environments and with some people better than others. For example, an active child will do less well in a restrictive, cramped environment and will therefore provoke more negative responses in adults, just as Tola's exuberance often brings him into conflict with his mother as he bumps into and knocks things over in their room.

Temperament

Temperament is genetically determined patterns of responding to the environment and to other people that persist through childhood and into adulthood (Schaffer 2006). These "constitutionally based individual differences' in behavioural style are 'emotional, motor and attentional reactivity and self-regulation' (Rothbart and Bates 1998: 105–76).

Thomas and Chess (1980) identified nine dimensions of temperament; within this, three types of children are identified:

- The easy child who responds positively to new events and has regular physical functions
- The difficult child who is irritable, has irregular patterns and responds negatively to new events
- The slow to warm up child who displays passive resistance and has few intense reactions positive or negative, but once adapted is more positive.

The key dimensions of these categories are:

- Activity level: frequency and vigour of movement
- Positive emotionality: sociability
- Inhibition and anxiety: fear and withdrawal in social interactions
- Negative emotionality: irritability and angry responses
- Effortful control/task persistence: staying focused

(Buss and Plomin 1984 and 1986)

From an interactionist perspective on development, temperament is mediated through the social experiences of the child. For example, a sociable child will elicit positive responses from caregivers, which in turn will encourage more sociable behaviour; of course this will also depend on the temperament of the adult. Thomas and Chess (1977, cited in Berk 2009: 423) talked about 'goodness of fit' wherein a child's and an adult's temperament may match or mismatch. For example, an outgoing, sociable adult might challenge a shy child, thereby encouraging more sociability, as we can see with Aisling and her father in the case study, while an equally shy adult may reinforce the child's shyness, thereby increasing it. This emphasizes the bi-directionality of children's development; who they are influences others' responses, which in turn influence the child's sense of self (Schaffer 2006). In this transactional model, there may be genetic 'pre-dispositions' but temperament is not fixed; it is shaped, strengthened or counteracted through relationships, experiences and cultural norms. Our personalities therefore are not entirely genetically determined by temperament; rather, temperament is 'the matrix from which later child and adult personality develops' (Ahadi and Robarth 1994: 190).

Dispositions

Lilian Katz (1995) maintains that there is a distinction between pre-dispositions that are present in our genetic make-up at birth and dispositions:

those which are learnt. She defines dispositions as a pattern of behaviour exhibited frequently and in the absence of coercion: a habit of mind under conscious and voluntary control (Katz 1995). It is this emphasis on learned behaviour and voluntary control that differentiates dispositions from temperament.

Both Katz (1995) and Dowling (2010) discuss the importance of developing positive dispositions to learning such as curiosity, intrinsic motivation and perseverance. They emphasize that dispositions are learned in subtle, unconscious ways and that once lost, are almost impossible to regain. Dowling (2010) outlines that one way in which young children's positive dispositions are enhanced or damaged is through the pedagogical approach in early childhood settings. But of course, by 2 years old children have already developed early dispositions at home, through their senses, emotions and interactions with their family. In the earlier case studies we can see how Tola's mother encourages her son's disposition to be curious while Aisling's mother reinforces her caring disposition. But for both of these children, like all others, it is the interactions within a child's secure attachment relationships which underpin their positive dispositions to life and love as well as learning (Siegel 1999).

Learning about self, life and love within the family

Donald Winnicott describes how a child's 'inherited potential' develops into an individual personality through the 'good enough' physical and emotional responsiveness of the caring adult (Winnicott 1960). Through providing a sensitive 'holding environment' the carer allows the child to pass to a state of greater autonomy and independence at their own pace. This means that a child who usually experiences consistent and prompt responses to their needs, can remain confident in the face of small instances of disillusionment when their carer is not immediately available (Winnicott 2005). This leads to a sense of 'ordinary specialness' (Kohut 1977, cited in Bateman and Holmes 1995). In this way, young children who experience loving responses from their caring adults develop positive ideas of themselves as being worthwhile and valuable. They also develop a positive view of close relationships as satisfying and enjoyable. These children develop confident and interested dispositions to exploring and learning about the world around them and also seem to be able to manage failure, 'bouncing back' from disappointment and frustration because their close attachment relationships with their parents provide them with 'an important resource for navigating stressful life events' (Osborne 2004: 5).

Attachment theory (John Bowlby 1907–1990)

Bowlby developed the theory of attachment from the idea that human babies have a biological need to have a close loving bond with their mother or caregiver, not only for physical survival but also for positive mental health. He stressed that it is the security and sense of safety provided by the parent that are the foundations of emotional attachment. In Bowlby's view, if this bond isn't allowed to form or is broken, emotional and personality development will be disrupted. Attachment, then, relates to the state and quality of an individual's emotional links to another person.

Bowlby (1988: 121) suggests that the framework for mother- (or other-) infant attachment is the coordination of 'care seeking' and 'care giving'. Attachment behaviours such as care or proximity seeking are triggered by separation or threatened separation from someone with whom the child has an attachment relationship. This separation anxiety is eased by gaining proximity; this might range from just being in sight or hearing soothing words to the physical closeness of being held. Responsive 'care giving' behaviours from the adult, that are complementary to the child's attachment behaviours and that are focused on maintaining the stability of the relationship, provide the child with a 'secure base' (see Chapter 8). Through these interactions the child gradually forms what Bowlby described as an internal working model of the attachment figure, which helps sustain the child for periods when they are separated from this person. This model also sets a 'blueprint' for what they can expect from close relationships and is thereby used to recreate and predict later relationships (Holmes 1993).

Where a parent or other caregiver offers a high degree of sensitivity and is generally responsive to a child's needs through engaging in consistent patterns of behaviour, the child will usually develop a secure attachment to them (Holmes 1993).

Ainsworth et al. (1978) identified that attachment relationships can also be insecure because the adult is unavailable, inconsistent or rejecting.

Not every parent is able to foster secure attachment relationships with their children, who may then experience mis-attuned or inconsistent responses to their needs. These children may learn to expect little from close relationships and may have low self-esteem (Lawrence 2006). This negative self-image is then often reinforced in their early years setting or later school setting as they may have difficulty in concentrating and learning (Lawrence 2006). Allan Schore (2001) identifies how the quality of a child's attachment affects their ability to regulate their emotions. He suggests that usually self-regulation is a combination of auto-regulation (without others) and interactive regulation (through interaction with others) but that people with insecure attachment patterns will either be always auto-regulating or always regulating interactively. This may become apparent in a setting when a child is either very demanding and seeks attention and emotional support in socially unacceptable ways or may make very few demands and thereby be overlooked. A child who feels good about themselves and has a strong sense of belonging will feel able to approach their caring adult, confident that they will get their needs met.

For 2-year-olds who are coping with high levels of difficulty in their home environments, the emotional stress they are experiencing may be manifested through quite contrasting behaviours such as clinging or running around manically, as they may simultaneously be relieved to be somewhere else but also very anxious about being away from their home and their parent. These children may also be continuously on alert for negative responses from others and, because they have learned this pattern of response, may also instigate and provoke negative interactions. The continuously high levels of anxiety they are experiencing means that they are more frequently in 'fight or flight' mode and dangerous levels of cortisol will be continuously present in their brains, which can have a damaging effect on their brain development and ability to focus and learn (Gerhardt 2004).

In this way, the 'internal working model' of relationships that children have developed at home will impact on how they interpret and respond to relationships with their Key Person in the setting, so Key Persons need to be able to adjust their responses in a way that will reassure the child. Practitioners should remember that by responding promptly and positively to a child's needs and by offering consistency and continuity of experience, they will be contributing an additional or alternative component to that child's mental model of relationships. In this way, practitioners in early years settings can add to the factors that enable children's resilience because the child has someone else in their lives who respects them and in whom they can trust. However, it remains that the most influential factor in children's future well-being is the establishment of a secure attachment in their family and that their repertoire of strategies to regulate their emotions and deal with anxiety is largely influenced by the emotional climate of children's early home life (Colman et al. 2006, cited in Berk 2009).

Parenting styles and their influence on development

The Irish playwright George Bernard Shaw (1984: 25) said 'Perhaps the greatest social service that can be rendered by anyone to the country and to mankind is to bring up a family', a sentiment that echoes through current political rhetoric, to the degree that *how* people bring up a family has become the focus of much debate, criticism and research.

Most discussions on effective parenting reflect Baumrind's far-reaching research, which identifies four different styles of parenting and their effects on children's behaviour and outcomes (1966). These different parenting styles are characterized by their disciplinary strategies, the degree of warmth and nurturance in the relationship, their communication styles and different expectations of children according to their maturity. In Baumrind's view, the most effective parenting is characterized by parents who are caring, attentive, responsive, cooperative and warm and who use child-friendly and age-appropriate disciplinary methods. These parents use what she calls an 'Authoritative' approach, wherein they set and monitor clear standards of behaviour and use supportive reasoning rather than punitive discipline (Baumrind 1991). Maccoby (1992) suggests that the children in these families develop into capable and successful people; they tend to have well-developed self-regulation and social cooperation skills because their parents have modelled assertiveness coupled with negotiation within their relationship.

In contrast, children of parents who expect their orders to be obeyed without explanation may become obedient and proficient but they tend to have less social competence and lower self-esteem. This 'obedience and status-oriented' approach to parenting is termed 'Authoritarian' (Baumrind 1991: 62). The opposite approach to this is 'Permissive' parenting, wherein parents are lenient and make few demands on their children in terms of their behaviour. Although this approach may come from a benign intention not to impose their will on their children, it requires children to learn how to self-regulate on their own, which many fail to do, resulting in poor educational outcomes and a low degree of happiness. An extreme version of this is the 'Uninvolved' parenting style, in which not only do the parents make few demands, they also do not communicate or respond fully to their children. Even though these parents will usually meet their child's basic needs, this approach can result in neglect.

However, as in all aspects of human development, paths are not linear and causality is not always direct; so it is with the influence of parenting styles. For example, in two-parent families one parent may adopt an authoritative style while the other has a more permissive approach, thereby creating a unique blend in their family. Also, the child's character and any particular physical or learning need will influence parents' approach to discipline and expectations of behaviour; in this way, a particular parenting style may not necessarily result in the predicted outcomes.

Parenting styles can also be moderated between different generations and cultural shifts. For example Adetutu, in the case study, says that some of the older 'Aunties' think she is too soft with Tola; they expect children to learn instant obedience, which conflicts with her approach. Understanding socio-cultural contexts is important as what is recognized as effective parenting differs and the outcomes of 'authoritative' parenting that may be seen in white middle-class children may not hold true for children from minority ethnic and economically disadvantaged groups, where the impact of poverty, stereotyping and discrimination in wider society will also impact on children's future life chances (Garcia and Garcia 2009). There are also changing life circumstances that are common across all social groups, such as divorce, unemployment, chronic illness or having a child with a disability, which will impact on the ability to parent effectively. As Roberts et al. say, 'When mothers' and fathers' own well-being is under threat then their capacity to parent successfully diminishes' (2009: 13). This is particularly acute where there is maternal depression or domestic violence; children in these environments are very vulnerable and their future outcomes are compromised (Barker et al. 2012). But it should be remembered that although there is a link between poverty, parental stress and parenting skills, individual parents react in different ways, depending on their temperament, their own experiences of being parented and the degree to which they are supported by family and the community (Katz et al. 2007; The Strategy Unit and DfES, 2008).

It seems from this that the issues involved in effective parenting and its impact on children's development are complex and that most parents may need support, advice and guidance at some point in their parenting career. Yet in the extension of the entitlement to free early education for 2-year-olds in 2010, the families who are seen to be in need of such guidance are those that are categorized as 'disadvantaged', and initially this was defined in relation to income, that is, children eligible for free school meals (DFE 2011). The National Centre for Social Research report that, 'The programme aims to provide good quality early education combined with support for parents, for example, to improve their confidence in supporting their children's learning and to deal with other challenges in their lives, such as health problems and family difficulties' (DFE 2011: 5).

These laudable aims surely mark a positive change towards support for parents in the UK, yet if based on a deficit view of 'disadvantaged' families and a 'one-size-fits-all' approach to parenting, while ignoring the wider issues such as poverty and employment, then the effectiveness of the focus on parenting programmes as a remedy for families' problems and children's outcomes is questionable (Waldfogel 2004).

This isn't to say that parenting programmes may not be helpful; indeed there is some evidence to suggest that they can contribute to maternal mental health (Barlow et al. 2002). Also, there is an expressed desire amongst parents for advice and support (Family Lives 2014). However, there is concern that where that advice and support are not tailored to respond to particular parents' needs and concerns, then it obscures the different positions that parents hold in society, treating parents as a homogeneous group rather than as individuals with a particular socio-cultural context.

It could also be argued that being a parent is becoming increasingly professionalized, as the 'parenting industry' produces more and more 'expert' guidance, thereby undermining parents' confidence in their role (Guldberg 2009). So, although being offered information about how babies and young children grow and learn can be illuminating and helpful for parents, this should most usefully be combined with opportunities to observe and reflect on their child and to share concerns and ideas. This reflects the 'Gerber Approach' to parent education, which is based on the work of Emmi Pikler and her 'respectful' care of infants (Petrie and Owen 2005; Owen and Petrie 2006) in which small groups of parents whose children are the same age, spend time watching their children at play and, with the facilitation of two practitioners (one of whom is focused on the children and one who facilitates the discussion) they talk about what they see and then reflect on their responses. This approach not only ensures that each parent's particular concerns are addressed but that their own expertise in their knowledge of their child is respected.

Partnership: views of family and family values

The kind of respect for parents' wisdom that is present in both the Gerber approach (Owen and Petrie 2005) and the approach of the Pen Green Centre in 'Involving Parents in their Children's Learning' (Whalley and the Pen Green Centre Team 2007) is what is required of all early childhood practitioners as they build effective partnership relationships with families. However, although practitioners identify this aspect of their practice as essential to young children's well-being, there seems to also be an underlying critical view of parents, who are often perceived to be either more interested in their work than in spending time with their child, or ill-informed and incapable of meeting their child's needs (Manning-Morton 2014). Given that comments about the 'problem' of poor parenting are made in the media with great frequency and that there is an emphasis in policy discussions on the need to address economic and social issues through 'better' parenting, it is perhaps not surprising that such 'parent blaming' is absorbed into early childhood practitioners' thinking. However, you cannot hold negative, deficit views of parents on one hand and expect them to be involved in the life of the nursery and their children's learning on the other (Whalley and the Pen Green Centre Team 2007), so practitioners need to reflect on their views of families and on how their own experiences and values may impact negatively on positive partnership working.

Reflective exercise

What does the word 'family' mean to you? Who do you include in your 'family'; people related to you genetically, socially, by law, proximity or by another aspect of relationship?

What are your views of different kinds of families? Note down three words that immediately come to mind when thinking about:

- Large families with four or more children
- Travelling families
- Families with same sex parents
- Families where children are sent away to school
- Single parent families
- Foster families.

Your notes may reveal where you hold particular views or prejudices, so a necessary place to start is for practitioners to consider their views of different kinds of family structure. Clark (2010) argues that the dominant idea of the 'nuclear family' – that is, a heterosexual adult couple with dependent children – has become idealized and has informed policy and practice in the UK, even though this family form does not represent the majority of families internationally nor is it necessarily the best form of family. Often, ideas about what makes a 'proper' family are justified by claims that such family forms will produce better outcomes for children. For example, a dominant idea is that children need a mother and a father for healthy psychological development. However, Golombok (2000) argues that what matters in terms of children's health and well-being is not the structure but the quality of the relationships within the family. Children of lesbian parents, for example, are no more likely to grow up to be gay, be confused about their sexuality or have difficulties at school (a common set of beliefs) than the children of heterosexual parents. Golombok also highlights issues of social inequality as being as much the root cause of family difficulties as family structure. For example, while children from certain types of families (such as children from single parent families) may experience higher rates of problems, this is more likely to be related to the fact that single parent families are more likely to be living in poverty and often face discrimination (Golombok 2000).

Therefore, there is not one way that a family 'should' be and early childhood settings should ensure that their policies, procedures and practices reflect this, for example, by changing admissions forms from 'Mother's name' and 'Father's name' to 'Parent's name' and reconsidering whether and how you celebrate Mother's Day and Father's Day – how do children who don't have a mother or father present in their lives feel about this? It would be useful for practitioners to think about 'who are the people around this child, who interact with them and affect how they are?' This may give a more inclusive view of who is significant in the child's family.

Practitioners also need to think deeply about their own ideas about those approaches to parenting they feel comfortable with, agree with and value and those they do not. If partnership is to be based on mutual respect, then it must be acknowledged that there will be different perspectives but through listening to each other, practitioners and parents can work towards better collaboration. This is not easy, however. Although practitioners and parents do develop warm, supportive relationships, there are ever-present underlying issues of power, which, unless thought about explicitly, can set a particular tone to the relationship or even severely undermine it. Differences of class, ethnicity, gender, sexual identity and disability can affect the power relations between the parent/carer and practitioner. In addition, the circumstances in which families have come to use the setting will influence their view of and approach to their relationships with practitioners and vice versa.

Families' circumstances and feelings may include any of the following:

- Parents who have been expected to bring their child to a setting due to concerns about their parenting or the child's development may feel wary or defensive.
- Parents whose child has an identified disability or special need may be concerned about their child receiving the type of care they need.
- Parents whose cultural group or family unit is in a minority in the setting may feel anxious about lack of recognition and possible discrimination.
- Parents who are used to feeling competent in their professional lives but are unsure about their parenting may fear being undermined or usurped by the practitioner.
- Parents may have health or family issues that they fear may be misunderstood by practitioners and therefore will not disclose them.

Any of the above situations may lead parents to be reticent in sharing information or to over-inflate their child's abilities in the hope that saying the right thing will gain the practitioner's approval and acceptance of their child. For example, it was a long while before Adetutu in the case study mentioned their accommodation problems and low income to Tola's Key Person, who then realised why Tola was absent on the days they had trips or events for which parents had to contribute money or materials; this led the nursery to rethink how these events were organized. These are particularly important issues for settings moving from working with families in one particular social class or group to expanding their intake of children from families with a different socio-economic and cultural context, as is the case for many settings in the private sector expanding to cater for funded 2-year-olds. It is unhelpful for practitioners to generalize about parents/carers both within and between cultural groups, as they will have a variety of different family and cultural values. This will include what is important in life, what behaviour is acceptable, their world-view, how ideas are expressed and interactions in relationships, as well as the more obvious issues such as clothes, diet and religious beliefs.

Reflective exercise

At the end of a working day, make some notes on all the interactions you and your colleagues have had with parents and other family members.

- Did you balance your professional knowledge with the family's understanding of the child?
- Did you receive family members' questions with openness and interest or defensiveness?
- Have you heard any judgemental views about parents expressed by colleagues?
- Have you or a colleague used professional jargon that families are less familiar with?
- Have you or your setting made any changes as a result of parents' suggestions?
- How are differences of opinion about childcare settled?
- Who makes decisions about what happens in the setting and who has the authority to make these decisions?

However, as Brooker (2010) points out, power imbalances can work both ways with middle-class, professional parents exercising power over practitioners, whose professional qualifications and skilled work they may not value. But, although these parents may be perceived as freely choosing their childcare arrangements, the decision and choices parents/carers make about childcare are complex. The Families, Children and Childcare Study (Leach 2006) found that few of the parents who want non-maternal care get the type they wanted and many find themselves using the type they wanted least. The study suggests that there are links between parents' satisfaction with the childcare they are using and their 'ideal' childcare (Barnes et al.

2006). This requires that practitioners acknowledge and address the feelings that parents have about how they have come to be in their particular setting, in order to work positively together in the future.

Practitioners must also take into account that *all* parents will have ambivalent feelings about leaving their child and they will all have concerns and expectations about the relationships their child will form with their Key Person and others in the setting. Goldschmied and Selleck (1996) discuss the complex feelings that are aroused in the triangle of care between practitioner, parent and child, which, if not effectively addressed and contained, can result in difficult practitioner–parent relationships rather than mutually respectful ones. Feelings of anxiety, rivalry, guilt, doubt and loss can be rife in this triangular relationship so creating a 'triangle of trust' (Goldschmied and Selleck 1996) through clear, respectful communication is of paramount importance. For example, a year after leaving the nursery, a colleague bumped into the parent of one of her former key children. The two adults had shared a trusting and mutually respectful relationship, so it was surprising when the parent confessed during their conversation that she had felt the need to sometimes wash her son's clothes at the end of the day so they no longer smelled of the practitioner's perfume!

Vincent and Ball suggest that parents' and practitioners' communications can be hampered; 'mothers by their emotional involvement with the children which makes them wish to preserve untroubled relationships with carers for the children's sake, and carers by their reluctance to risk being seen as uncaring and "in it for the money"' (2006: 130). Therefore, they argue that there is always potential for conflict and antagonism between parents and practitioners.

These conflicts and antagonisms can arise from the different and varied expectations parents will have of settings and from differences in childcare approach between parent and practitioner. Issues such as setting limits and managing behaviour, gender roles, toilet learning and many others are all potential areas of disagreement (Manning-Morton and Thorp 2003, 2006; Goldschmied and Jackson 2004). Negotiating these differences is an interpersonal skill that is essential in the effective early childhood practitioner, who needs to tread a line between accommodating parents' wishes as far as possible (a setting manager calls this the 'why not?' response to all situations) and negotiating other aspects in an attitude of respect and understanding, while ensuring that the ethos and principles of the setting's agreed approach are not undermined (assuming that parents have been involved in developing these principles in the first place). Where settings do not adequately consider these concerns, communication between busy and often stressed parents and practitioners can break down.

Lawson (2003), cited in Fitzgerald (2004), explains partnership as the process of information sharing and communication. This is not about just informing parents of what is happening; it is about involving parents in the life of the setting and their children's learning. Robson (1996: 61–5) suggests that more direct involvement of parents in their children's activities can produce a range of gains: for children's achievements; for enhancement of parents' and practitioners' knowledge, skills and confidence; and for minimizing conflicting behaviour between home and setting.

She also asserts that settings need to be accountable to parents, a view that is supported in the latest version of the Early Years Foundation Stage (DFE 2014a), which includes some specific instructions as to what practitioners are required to do in this regard. However, such instructions cannot equip the practitioner with the high level of interpersonal sensitivity and respect required to develop effective partnership working. These skills and reflective practices need to be a central focus of regular supervision sessions as well as integral to qualification and further professional development training in the early years field.

Conclusion

As Susan Golombok points out, the journey to becoming who we are is a complex one, she says:

> A major lesson to be learned from longitudinal research is that some children arrive in the same place by following the same route, some follow different routes to reach the same destination, some set out along the same route but branch off to arrive in different places, and others follow pathways that never meet. Although parents cannot determine the routes their children will take, they can influence them in one direction or another.
>
> (Golombok 2000: 103)

This chapter has highlighted some of the key aspects of the personality development of 2-year-olds and the impact of parenting styles and families' socio-cultural contexts on their developing self-concept. Above all, it has emphasized the importance of practitioners reflecting on their values and attitudes towards families in order to develop effective partnerships. Parents can experience early years care and education for their 2-year-old as a joy and a support or they can experience it as a time of anxiety and conflicting feelings. Often they will experience a bit of both of these, so practitioners need as clear an understanding as possible of what the issues might be for a parent/carer and to develop good communication and interpersonal skills to carry out this crucial aspect of practice effectively.

2 Setting out: transitions and change

Introduction

A 2-year-old is at the beginning of learning how to move out into the world with self-assurance and hopefully with a belief that they can look to others for assistance when required. This kind of confidence and well-being comes from the security of their relationships within their family and with a Key Person in the early years setting. This chapter emphasizes that the careful implementation of the Key Person Approach (Elfer et al. 2011) through child-centred settling-in processes is a crucial feature of effective practice and provision for 2-year-olds who are newly setting out on their journey of discovery of the early years setting and beyond. Alicia Lieberman also emphasizes these aspects when she suggests that:

> A successful child-care experience calls for careful attention to three major aspects of non-parental care: the daily transitions of departing and re-uniting, the quality of the child's emotional experiences in the course of the day, and the quality of the parents' relationship with the caregivers. These three factors remain important regardless of where the child-care arrangement takes place.
>
> (Lieberman 1995: 203)

Case studies

Elly (2y2m) is two weeks into the settling-in period and so is staying just for half days without her mother. When she arrives, most of the group are having a song time. Toyin, her Key Person, moves toward Elly and her mother and greets them both by name. She is smiling and chatting softly because Elly's mother has explained that Elly likes quieter, non-physical approaches. Toyin brings a chair for Elly's mother to sit on, Elly sits at her feet on the floor and Toyin sits nearby, also on the floor. As the songs continue, Toyin sings the words and does the actions really clearly as she sees that Elly is watching her. She makes no attempt to get Elly to join in, allowing her to acclimatize to the situation. Elly sees 'Hello Kitty', a soft toy, nearby and reaches for it. Holding it on her lap she moves it slightly to the music. After five minutes, Elly's mother explains she has to go to the post office and will be back at lunchtime. Elly stands up, drops Kitty and, frowning, follows her mother. Toyin goes to the door too. They have a pre-arranged routine of a 'big hug' then Toyin lifting Elly so she and her mother can kiss either side of the glass window in the door. Toyin and Elly return to the group and Elly picks up Kitty again. Later that morning Toyin notices that Elly is taking Kitty with her as she moves around the room but when her mother returns, Kitty is discarded. She makes a note to make sure that Kitty available for Elly when she comes tomorrow.

* * *

Leyla (2y4m) is in her third week too. She is one of three children; her brother came to this setting but has now moved on to school. Leyla was very confident at the home visit when she showed Andy (her Key Person) around her flat and all her toys. She played with the collection of purses he brought with him and kept the one with a chain shoulder strap over the weekend. She now often walks around with it in the setting. As soon as they arrive in the morning, Leyla runs in to show Andy whatever she has brought with her each day. She launches herself at him (which has resulted in a few bumps) and then runs off into the garden. Andy is trying to devise a less risky way of greeting! Her only 'wobble' was on a day he was off sick, when Leyla physically fought off any attempts by Toyin (her co-Key Person) to comfort her. Andy and Toyin are planning ways to help Leyla feel comfortable with Toyin in a few weeks when she is a bit more settled. Meanwhile, Andy is offering her as much consistency as possible.

The experience of separation

In Chapter 1 we discussed 'care seeking' as a key feature of attachment relationships (Bowlby 1988: 121) that is, behaviour that results in a child maintaining proximity to their trusted adult. Here we will consider how that behaviour is triggered by potential separation, then becomes more intense and other attachment behaviours emerge when separation becomes real. It is an unavoidable fact that forming close loving relationships with others brings joy in that person's company but also sadness when they are absent. These are the two sides of the attachment coin: attachment on one side and separation and loss on the other. So, when a child starts in an early childhood setting for the first time and has to be without their parent/carer, separation and loss are at the centre of the experience.

Separation and loss (John Bowlby 1907–1990)

As a result of his studies of troubled adolescents who had experienced traumatic separations such as bereavement and abandonment, Bowlby suggested that any elective separation between mother and child in the first three years should be avoided, as he saw prolonged separation as the cause of later psychological disturbance. However, he also agreed that 'an affectionate, stable person who will act as a substitute mother over a period of years' (Karen 1998: 319) is what is required in any absence of the mother. Other researchers, such as Rutter and Rutter (1993) and Rutter (1995) found that although prolonged early separation can result in negative outcomes, factors such as temperament, disability, severe family discord and maternal depression can be even more damaging to mental and emotional health. The work of Bowlby and the films of the Robertsons (Robertson and Robertson 1953) clearly show the high level of distress and the process of loss that young children go through when separated from their parents. This process includes recognizable phases of yearning, searching, anger, despair and denial, which reflect the processes that grieving adults also experience after bereavement (Holmes 1993).

So, children's separation from their familiar and loved adults should be taken very seriously. When a young child, who is still physically and emotionally vulnerable and dependent, is separated from those they know and trust to protect them and help them survive, their primary response is to protest, using whatever means they have to try to keep that person near to them. Active distress behaviours such as crying, screaming and shouting, biting and kicking or even being sick are all common responses to being left. Bowlby (1973) emphasized that this is a normal response when an attachment bond is threatened. After a period of time though, the child will begin to despair of being able to make their attachment figure return and fall into apathy punctuated by crying (Lieberman 1995). For example, in the case study scenario, Elly cried at the initial separation but soon stopped; however, Toyin noticed that she did not really play so she freed herself up from other tasks to spend more time with her and then devised the goodbye routine with Elly's mother. If, unlike Elly, a child isn't given support from a consistent and caring person during this phase, the child may enter a state of detachment. In this phase the child can be seen seeking contacts with any adult available, which may be wrongly interpreted by practitioners as evidence of the child being settled or of their independence. However, close observation would reveal that these contacts are superficial, indiscriminate and transitory and do not constitute the kind of secure relationship with their Key Person necessary for them to become *healthily* independent in the setting.

As a result of Bowlby's and the Robertsons' work, it was found that the effects of separation could be mitigated by commonsense measures, for example, in hospitals more frequent visits by parents, the child having introductory visits to the ward and taking in familiar comforting toys. These strategies will be familiar to early childhood practitioners who implement 'settling-in' policies in their settings. Hospitals also introduced 'named nurse' practices, which are similar to key working in early years settings, whereby a practitioner has primary responsibility for the care of a small group of children and their families. For example, in the case study scenario, Elly's mother said how reassured she felt that Toyin was her Key Person and that she had been so honest with her about Elly not playing and appreciated how much thought Toyin had put into making Elly feel more secure. Such practices are of fundamental importance in supporting 2-year-olds making the transition into early childhood settings and are the focus of the rest of this chapter.

Transitions

Transitions can be thought of as all the changes that take place in children's lives. Here though, we are focusing on the change between a 2-year-old mostly being at home with known and trusted family to spending much time away in a childcare and education setting with people who, at first, are strangers. Two-year-olds are finding out about who they are, are still developing their attachment models and learning about how relationships work; they also feel their emotions very intensely. Therefore, it is important that practitioners plan transitions so that children will see themselves as worthwhile people, with a positive sense of belonging, who know that these new adults are 'on their side'. They will know this when their wishes, needs and feelings are listened to and they are provided with a 'safe haven' from the rough seas of separation through the establishment of a caring relationship in the setting (Holmes 2014: 56).

This requires developing settling-in processes that are child-centred. It certainly does not mean having a rigid set time period in which the child is expected to settle, or seeing the settling-in as only happening after the parent leaves (as described by some practitioners). Rather, it means ensuring that from the start, parents, children and Key Persons spend significant amounts of time together in the setting so they can come to know each other well.

Manning-Morton and Thorp (2006) say that the main aim of the settling-in process is to minimize the distress of the child by helping them to make a new relationship with the Key Person, while gradually separating from their parents. But each child and family will have different needs and responses to this process and for some young children this may take a very long time. On the other hand there are children, perhaps like Leyla in the case study scenario, who seem to take separation more in their stride. Whether this is because they feel so secure in the knowledge of their parents' return and continuing love that they do not have to worry, or whether it is an avoidant response to having learned that they cannot rely on anyone, it is probably hard to say at first. But by learning about the child and family alongside the parent over a period of time, the practitioner can fine-tune their interactions with the child according to their unique personalities and needs. The resulting increased sensitivity of the practitioner enables the creation of a relationship between Key Person and child that will mitigate the discomfort and distress of their parent's departure. Given the potential differences in needs and responses of children and their parents at this time, it is clear that there is no one plan for settling all children. The important thing is to have a plan that is based on child-centred principles and is open and flexible enough to take into account differing needs.

Implementing transitions that match the characteristics of 2-year-olds

Although some older children may cope better with the adventure of starting in an early years setting, for most 2-year-olds this is a very stressful time. They are in a strange and perhaps overwhelming environment, meeting several new children and adults, encountering unfamiliar toys and experiences, and then their most important person leaves them for reasons they can only vaguely understand. These situations are all made particularly difficult because of the key characteristics of 2-year-olds' development.

First, they are establishing a concept of themselves as separate, active and autonomous people, yet are still dependent on others. They are at an important point of learning about how to balance their desire to be a separate person and move away yet still retain the love and closeness of their close relationships. So starting at a setting may be an experience that is outside a 2-year-old's zone of emotional understanding and could be interpreted by the child as a rejection or abandonment. These unconscious fears may be expressed by the child rejecting the Key Person and their parent through overt defiant behaviour or through more indirect behaviours such as refusing food. Both parents and practitioners will need support with reflecting on, understanding and providing for these potential protest behaviours. This can happen through good communication with each other and, for the practitioner, regular opportunities for reflective supervision with a manager or colleague. In this way the adults can aim to make this experience a positive challenge in which a 2-year-old can learn that change can happen and they remain intact emotionally, rather than a negative trauma that teaches them that change is dangerous. Alicia Lieberman suggests that,

> When toddlers can separate from their parents with a sadness that is manageable, they are more able to engage with other people than if they are overcome by distress. Conversely, enjoying the child-care setting can help to relieve the toddlers' apprehension when the parent leaves.
>
> (Lieberman 1995: 203)

A key element that will support positive learning here is the child coming to know that they can rely on the new adult, so any absence of the Key Person during this time should be avoided if at all possible and if they do have to be away, then the child and parent must be kept fully informed.

In addition, 2-year-olds often feel out of control but strive to retain control over whatever they can. They want things to stay as much the same as possible, often being set in their ways and needing to follow set rituals in their day to help them feel secure. Therefore, making sure that there are familiar items from home in the setting for when the child first arrives and agreeing (and following) parting rituals such as described in the case study are important supportive practices. A 2-year-old's self-concept is also highly influenced by the messages they receive about how they and their family are valued, so ensuring that the child's ethnicity, their home culture and family structure are all represented in displays, artefacts and play materials must be high on practitioners' agenda.

Second, the language and social skills of 2-year-olds are still quite immature, so verbally communicating their needs to unfamiliar adults and children is difficult. But by spending good amounts of time with the parent and child, the Key Person can learn about how the child communicates, any idiosyncratic words or particular gestures they have, key words in their home language and favourite sayings, songs and stories that are used at particular times or events. The Key Person can also, alongside the parent, introduce them to one or two other children who perhaps share a particular interest and support them in playing together.

Third, 2-year-olds are making huge gains in their cognitive understanding but understanding time is not yet established. This means that they may think (or want to think) that because their parent stays in this new place with them at first, they will always stay with them, as Elly did in the case study scenario. So however difficult it may be for the adults involved, parents and practitioners must be honest about this with the child, telling them something like, 'Mummy will stay and play with the sand with you, then she will go and have a cup of tea while you and I play on the bikes outside, then she will come and take you home'. Obviously the phrasing will be adapted to suit the particular situation but it is important to always use a concrete event such as 'after lunch' rather than 'later' to describe when their parent will return and to repeat this simple description as many times as is needed during the separation.

Lastly, many 2-year-olds are at the point of their physical development when they are learning to control their bowels and bladder and use the toilet rather than nappies. Some 2-year-olds may have already accomplished this learning, although parents should not be surprised if the child cannot maintain this control during their transition into a setting. Unfortunately top-down pressure in settings that are more used to working with older children means that parents are sometimes pressurized into encouraging toilet learning before their child starts, which, if premature for their child, is only likely to cause difficulties. Similarly, expecting a child to undertake toilet learning at the same time as getting to know the setting and Key Person is unreasonable. It is better to wait until the child is settled and the Key Person and parent can then work together to plan this learning according to the child's readiness.

Building bridges between home and setting

In addition to all these expected stresses, some children may have other anxieties too, which the practitioner needs to know about in order understand the child's behaviours.

Reflective exercise

List all the different circumstances you can think of in which a 2-year-old might be making a transition into your setting.
You may have included some of the following:

- Their family might have recently migrated from another country. This might be for positive economic/professional reasons or to escape difficult or traumatic events in their home country. But whatever the reason, the child will be coping with a new home environment, new language, new foods, and so on.
- The child may have spent most of their time at home just with their parent/carer(s). This may have been a positive choice for the family or a default choice due to lack of work or inability to find employment.

- They may have previously attended another setting; either a childminder's home or a baby room at a centre. This may have been a positive or a negative experience for the child and/or parent. When 2-year-olds transition from one setting to another, practitioners need to pay as much attention to broadening their knowledge of that setting's approach and conferring with the previous practitioners as they do to liaising with the child's parents/carers.
- The child may have spent a lot of time with extended family either in their own home or at their grandparents, aunts, cousins, for example.
- The child may have been recently assessed as having an additional learning need, which the parent/carer is still coming to terms with.

Reflecting on this wide range of circumstances makes it clear why Manning-Morton and Thorp (2006) suggest that another purpose of the settling-in process is to build bridges between home and nursery. They emphasize that the 'bridge' must be crossed regularly and frequently by the practitioner and the parent from one side to the other, in order for the child's sense of well-being and belonging to be nurtured. It is the manner in which this crucial aspect of practice is carried out which, they suggest, not only impacts on the child's and parents' experience at the time, it also seems to set the tone for the future relationship between everyone involved. There are many practical ways in which the 'bridge' can be crossed. For example, students on Key Times courses have worked with parents to develop 'special boxes' where each child has a container in which they keep special and meaningful objects and pictures from home. The parents write down or tell the Key Person why these things are significant so they can be used in key group times for sharing stories or at times when the child needs to feel in touch with their home and family, thereby fulfilling a similar function to a child's 'transitional object' (Winnicott 2005: 6).

Transitional objects (Donald Winnicott 1896–1971)

Donald Winnicott, an English paediatrician and psychoanalyst, developed the idea of 'transitional objects' (Winnicott 2005). These objects are frequently blankets or soft toys but can also be other objects or even a song. A transitional object becomes important when a young baby first experiences a gap between a felt need and the satisfaction of that need (such as through a feed not being quite ready when they are hungry); they then begin to realize that they are a separate person. The resulting feelings of anxiety about being alone may be managed by the child through creating in their mind the comfort and support that their mother would otherwise give them, using the familiar feel and smell of a blanket or toy as a representation of this. What is important about these objects is that their sensory properties help the child to recall the parent in times of stress and so derive comfort and reassurance that their mother continues to exist in her absence. By the time the child is 2 years old, their transitional object may appear as a dirty smelly rag but to wash it would be to destroy their creation of motherliness.

Some 2-year-olds seem to choose a different toy to bring from home each day, and although these may not be transitional objects in the strict sense that Winnicott describes, they are still objects that are helping the child to manage the transition, just as Elly and Leyla both used objects to support themselves in the case study scenario. So expecting them to share it or taking it away to be 'put on the shelf' is to deprive the child of their own source of support. As well as ensuring young children have access to their own comforters whenever they wish, other ways of supporting them include having photographs of their family and friends displayed in profile books and inviting the parent and child to bring something familiar from home such as a music tape or their own potty, feeder cup or bottle.

A key way in which practitioners' understanding of individual families' contexts and concerns can be improved greatly is through undertaking a visit to the child's home before they start in the setting. These visits can also facilitate information sharing between parent and Key Person in a more relaxed setting, which can make it more likely that the parent has a chance to tell the Key Person about their child and their expectations of the setting rather than just answering a list of questions and facing a barrage of information on policies! Most importantly though, a home visit means that when the child does come to the setting, they will already have met their Key Person and the Key Person will have found out information about their interests that will enable them to prepare the environment and play opportunities that will help the child to feel at home and see this new place as interesting and exciting.

Greenman and Stonehouse (1996), Goldschmied and Jackson (2004) and Manning-Morton and Thorp (2003, 2006) all discuss these and a range of other strategies, which, if implemented sensitively, can make the early days of separating much less stressful, can increase parents'/carers' confidence in the quality of care their child is receiving and ease some of their ambivalent feelings as discussed below.

Parents separating from their children

Having reflected on the feelings and issues for children arising from separations, practitioners and students on Key Times courses are then asked to consider how parents might feel. They are often surprised to find that they identify the same feelings of loss, distress and confusion in the adults as they did in the children, occasionally mixed with relief and pleasure as described by a parent in the Key Times video:

> After a week or two, they sent me away from the nursery for about two or three hours which was hard but at the same time was absolutely blissful – because for the first time in five months I had three hours to myself! . . . but it was bitter-sweet and certainly when I started leaving him for full days . . . I did find it quite hard.
>
> (Manning-Morton and Thorp 2006 video)

There is one important different emotion experienced by the adults in this situation though: guilt, a constant companion to many parents who leave their child to be cared for by others. Although not all parents will feel guilty, the constant, ongoing debate about whether it is better for very young children to be cared for at home or whether they are more 'school ready' if they go to an early years setting, is bound to create uncertainty in the hearts of even the most confident parent as to whether they are doing the right thing for their child. This uncertainty and ambivalence can be transferred to the parent's feelings toward the Key Person (Page 2011). On the one hand, they want their child to like and feel safe with their Key Person but may also worry that they will then lose their child's love. For example, when parting and reuniting with their child, parents do not want their child to be upset but feel abandoned if their child does not protest on parting or ignores them when they return, as described by a parent in the Key Times video.

> Maybe part of me didn't want it to be possible, but I remember one day when I came in to pick Edie up and she didn't give me a second glance . . . I realize that this is a good thing now but at the time I was so cut up about it, I thought, 'Oh no! My daughter's forgotten me.' But it was a measure of how at home she was here.
>
> (Manning-Morton and Thorp 2006 video)

The Key Person's responsibility here is to support the relationship between the parent and child through supporting the parent–child interactions. Knowing when to withdraw into the background and when to step in, as Toyin did in the case study scenario, is a key professional skill. Effective practice in this area particularly requires managing the point of separation sensitively as set out in the Key Times framework (Manning-Morton and Thorp 2006) some of which is reproduced below.

Practice box

Key aspects of managing separations and reunions

- The Key Person being available to give as much attention as possible to children and parents/carers as they arrive
- Greeting both parent and child them by name (pronounced correctly and making sure that it is the name they are usually called by, which may be different to the name on the form)
- Providing familiar toys or play experiences that the child is interested in
- Being alert to the moment parents/carers want to leave and drawing alongside the child to join the play and support the separation through a definite handover from parent to practitioner and facilitate any supportive rituals they have developed for saying goodbye
- Senior staff being alert and available to give any support the parent might need after leaving their child
- Parent invited to telephone for reassurance during the day
- Preparing the child for reuniting with her/his parent/carer as this can be as emotionally delicate as separating. A parent/carer's comments such as 'she's paying me back for leaving her' or 'he likes it better here than at home' must be refuted. Early explanation during the settling-in period that a child may sometimes be rejecting of their parent when collected and that it is about the difficulty small children can have adjusting to change will prepare a parent/carer. They will then be less likely to make a negative interpretation of such behaviour.
- Giving the parent honest but tactful feedback about how their child has been, i.e. 'She cried for about ten minutes but I stayed sitting with her and as she calmed down was able to interest her in the goldfish. She helped me feed them, like she does at home and then we read the goldfish book together. She was then able to play as long as I was nearby and seemed reassured when I kept telling her that you were coming after snack time.'

Necessary management and organizational considerations

However committed they are to implementing the kind of child-centred settling-in processes described above, many practitioners working in group settings report that the organization of new admissions to the setting is managed more with concern for targets and finances rather than for the needs of the children. This, it seems, is often the result of top-down pressure passed from Government to local authorities to setting leaders, and can be identified clearly in the implementation of the expansion of funded places for 2-year-olds (DFE 2011). In early 2014, one practitioner reported to the authors that her setting had admitted 14 2-year-olds during January! Other practitioners consistently agonize over the effects of several concurrent admissions on the new child, the existing children, the parents and themselves. Indeed, when asked how she was coping, the practitioner in the example above replied that she had been away sick that week, which is really no surprise!

In consideration of all the issues set out in this chapter, leaders and managers of early years settings need to find a way of managing external expectations in a way that protects the needs of the children by following these guidelines:

Practice box

- Discuss and agree a settling-in policy and procedure that reflect the good practice set out in this chapter. This will help prevent poor decisions being made under pressure.
- Plan admissions far enough ahead so that parents/carers can organize their time and be in the setting for extended periods of time to ensure their child is settled.
- Plan admissions so that there is adequate time for individual children to be settled before another one starts.
- Plan allocations so that individual Key Persons aren't settling several new children in a short period of time.
- Ensure that detailed plans are made for gradual introductions to a new group or setting over a prolonged period of time that suits the child and their family.
- Coordinate the Key Person's shifts with the parent and child's arrival.
- Plan in sufficient staffing to enable the Key Person to focus on the new family.

(Manning-Morton and Thorp 2006)

Transitions within settings

If transitions can be thought of as all the changes that take place in children's lives, careful thought also needs to be given to transitions from one group to another within an early years setting, transitions between provision such as between a playgroup session and a childminder's home and transition between one part of the day and another.

Most adults when faced with a change situation will feel a mixture of many

---

Reflective exercise

In order to empathize better with 2-year-olds experiencing these daily upheavals, it is useful for practitioners to reflect on their own responses to change.

Note down your feelings and responses to change in your life.

You may feel threatened or excited, destabilized or positively challenged. You may defend your current stability at all costs, or analyse the viability of new possibilities before you consider them, or you might be someone who is always looking for new things to experience.

---

emotions such as anxiety, insecurity, challenge, confusion, anticipation, dread and excitement, as will children. Adults and children will also go through a process that includes shock, withdrawal, grief, acknowledgement and adaptation. Our behaviours will reflect how involved we feel in the change process, how much control we have and how we are supported through it: whether we feel someone is 'on our side' helping us to adjust. But equally, the ways in which we respond to change reflect our personalities, our previous experiences and have their roots in our early attachment relationships. This means that practitioners need to consider how they support 2-year-olds in managing changes and transitions of any kind; how do we show them that we are on their side?

Principally, 2-year-olds should have continuity and consistency of relationships with a Key Person and with their peer group over a prolonged period of time. Research shows that children are more likely to receive appropriate care-giving and activities when they have had the same key worker for over two to three years (Raikes 1993). Some settings address this issue by Key Persons moving with their key children through the centre as they get older.

But in some settings very young children are expected to change groups and Key Person as frequently as every six months and the authors regularly hear of situations where children are expected to change group and Key Person only a few months after settling in! Such situations should be avoided through the proper planning and administration of new places for children as described above but where children do need to change to a new group and Key Person, they need to have a well-planned and gradual transition time. Settling-in may seem less of an issue in these circumstances because practitioners across the groups know each other, the rooms and routines well. However, the child and the parents often do not have this knowledge so the more information and control children and parents have, the better able they will be to adjust to the change. These transitions must consider a 2-year-old's need to make a relationship with a new Key Person, their friendship bonds with other children in the group and their parent's need to be involved and fully informed (Manning-Morton, 2003). Practitioners should therefore take into consideration children's maturity, temperament and friendships as well as their age in deciding when a child should move. Sometimes even very young children provide additional mutual support for each other if two friends move into the same group together. Practitioners and parents should agree exactly when and how this transition will happen and a summary report on the child and other records should be shared with the parent and new Key Person. Then the Key Person and child can visit the new group for short periods of time gradually extending this as the child and new Key Person build a relationship and the child becomes familiar with the routines and environment of the new group.

Equally important is the consideration given to changes of environment and aspects of the daily routine as discussed in Chapter 3. In many group settings where there is a long day and practitioners work on a shift pattern, children often start and finish their days in a different part of the setting to their main group area. These kinds of adult-imposed changes should be kept to a minimum for 2-year-olds and where such arrangements are necessary, it is preferable for the 3- and 4-year-olds to make the move rather than the 0–3s.

Conclusion

Making the transition from home to an early years care and education setting is a major step in a 2-year-old's journey. To help them make that step with a positive self-concept intact and with a sense of challenge and adventure rather than dread and trauma, early childhood settings must develop the kind of child- and family-centred settling-in processes described in this chapter. In addition, practitioners need to consider the full range of situations and motivations of families in order for each child and family to have a sense of belonging in the setting. And, in turn, for Key Persons to be able to develop their skills and capacities to support children and families through this process, they need effective support from managers and colleagues.

3 The Key Person as companion and guide throughout the day

Introduction

In the previous chapter we established the importance of the Key Person building secure relationships with 2-year-olds and their families when implementing a child-centred settling-in process. In this chapter we discuss how the Key Person has a central role as a guide and interpreter as their key children navigate their way through the routines of the day and become familiar with the ways and customs of the setting. Because practitioners are steeped in the culture of the nursery setting, it can be easy to forget that how and why things are done in a particular way may be strange and confusing to children and families as they will very likely be different to how things are done at home. But when they have someone who will explain, guide and support them through the day, children's confidence and well-being will grow.

Case study

Rima's (Key Person) reflections on Ollie (2) sleeping at nursery for the first time:

During the settling-in period Ollie was sometimes very upset and wanted his Mummy; he needed a lot of reassurance. When he was distressed he wanted to sit in his buggy, which was a familiar and safe place for him, like a transitional object between home and nursery. I allowed him to do this and from the buggy he would watch the other children playing and then eventually join in with them. He would return to the buggy for comfort. When we were getting children ready for sleeping time, I said to Ollie, 'You seem tired. This is when tired children rest on their own special mats.' He answered 'No!' 'Oh, OK,' I reassured him. Ollie started to cry saying, 'Mummy'. I suggested we go into the sleep room where he would see Sam (2y5m) with whom he had played earlier. But Ollie said, 'No, Mummy!' I explained that Mummy would be back after a sleep, a play and when tea came. I asked what he wanted to do while were waiting for Mum. 'Sit down on my buggy,' he insisted. I put the buggy inside the sleep room. Ollie said, 'Not stay here. I want my mummy.' I asked Ollie if he wanted to sit in his buggy while we read a book. Ollie nodded his head in consent. I chose a book but Ollie said, 'I don't read book. I want my mummy.' Ollie was yawning. I said, 'You really miss your mummy, don't you?' He nodded. 'Poor Ollie, Mummy back after tea,' I said and started to rock the buggy and sing 'Twinkle, Twinkle Little Star' and Ollie fell asleep straight away. I was a bit worried that some might think me wrong to let a child sleep in a buggy, but sometimes you have to weigh up what's best for the child, even if it looks bad to others!

The Key Person approach, physical interactions and a positive sense of self

Under point 2.4 of the theme 'Positive Relationships' the EYFS framework states, 'A Key Person has special responsibilities for working with a small number of children, giving them the reassurance to feel safe and cared for and building relationships with their parents' (DCSF 2008c: 2.4). However, there is little in the Framework that describes how these responsibilities will be carried out, particularly in relation to the crucial experiences that occur during physical care activities. The Key Times Framework (Manning-Morton and Thorp 2006), however, not only takes the Key Person Approach as its central principle, but the authors also identify that babies and young children need high levels of continuity and consistency in their care experiences and relationships in order to develop a positive, integrated sense of self. Two-year-olds learn from all their experiences; this means that they learn from unplanned activities such mealtimes, as well as planned play activities. Very importantly, the learning that takes place at these times is mostly about themselves. Some neuro-scientists such as Colin Blakemore (1998) have suggested that this aspect of development is the main focus for the brain in the early years.

So, in all of a child's experiences, the question 'who am I?' is being answered in a range of ways but particularly through physical experience. In their earliest days babies become aware of where their bodies begin and their mother's/carer's ends through the touch of skin when being held. This, along with the physical experiences of suckling, digestion and defecation, is an infant's earliest experience of their physical self (Bateman and Holmes 1995). This early understanding of self continues as toddlers and 2-year-olds explore what their bodies can do and produce. Psychoanalytic theory suggests that the feeling states we experience in infancy remain within us and form part of the template for our developing personalities. Donald Winnicott (2005) identified that when a baby has the experience of their needs being consistently understood and responded to, then gradually over time they develop a coherent sense of self. Lisa Miller (1992) explains how this comes about through both the physical experiences of feeding, holding and changing and their emotional counterparts. So the physical feeling of being held in the carer's arms has also the emotional feeling of being safely supported and held in the carer's mind, while feeding consists not only of the act of giving and taking in of food but also of the giving and taking in of love. In this perspective, if the manner in which intimate physical care is carried out is different every time it happens because it is a different person doing it, the child cannot rely on the repeated patterns of sensory information that would otherwise help them make sense of their experience and thereby develop a consistent sense of self.

Two-year-olds therefore need consistent and predictable interactions in their physical care experiences through the day. It is also crucial that physical care is carried out sensitively and with respect. Feelings and thoughts are transmitted very strongly through the non-verbal communications of touch, voice tone, gesture, facial expression and body stance. Two-year-olds' spoken language may still be immature but they understand a lot about their relationships with others and how others see them through these physical interactions.

Reflective exercise

Spend some time reflecting on the last time you were physically handled by a professional person, such as a physiotherapist or beauty therapist. What were your feelings before, during and after your treatment? What made this experience positive or negative for you?

In order to better understand children's feelings, practitioners and students attending Key Times training courses are often asked to role play being a hospital patient, some of whom are treated well, others not. They identify a negative experience as rough, rejecting, ignoring, casual, dismissive and inattentive, which makes them feel unsafe, vulnerable, in the wrong, let down and angry. Their treatment leaves them feeling worthless as people and wanting to respond aggressively. In contrast, the other patients identify a positive experience as attentive, gentle, reassuring, respectful, calm, taking time and inclusive, which makes them feel content, secure, confident, worthwhile and trusting and willing to cooperate with their 'medic'!

When thinking about how this relates to children, the powerful position we are in as adults and how we can choose to use that power positively or negatively in our interactions become clear. Building trust through positive physical interactions is a fundamental aspect of developing healthy close relationships with children. So knowing the person caring for you and that person knowing you well are very important. Also, practitioners need to regularly reflect on how they might sound or appear to different children in their group, especially new children who haven't yet got to know them well enough to understand their body language. Two-year-olds will interpret the adult's non-verbal signals according to the templates they have already developed through their experiences during infancy and toddlerhood. For example, Sinead's mother is very softly spoken, so Kelly, her Key Person had to deliberately tone down her usually more exuberant call to come for 'Island Time' as it was making Sinead wary of accepting Kelly's invitation.

Physical care that supports 2-year-olds' well-being

In consideration of these issues, if we want 2-year-olds to develop an integrated sense of self and to feel worthwhile and valued, practitioners need to stop seeing physical care activities as 'routine' and unimportant. Settings need to abandon practices that treat the children as if they had identical needs, such as sitting all the children on the toilet or potty at the same time or changing nappies as if the children were on a conveyor belt at a factory. Instead, these times should be seen as important life-learning activities. Two-year-olds may not spend quite as much time in care routines as they did as infants but they are still frequently physically handled by people who are bigger than they are; particularly if they have a disability or special need. Physical care times are all precious times when the carer is frequently in a one-to-one situation with the child, with fantastic opportunities for conversation and relationship building. Planning to use these routine times as creatively as possible and taking the opportunity to focus on the individual child is an essential part of supporting children's positive sense of self and therefore integral to developing a holistic curriculum (Manning-Morton and Thorp 2006).

Greenman and Stonehouse call their book *Prime Times* to signify the importance of physical care in the child's life in a day care setting. They define excellence in this area:

> Caring times are individualised, relaxed, gentle, full of conversation and self-help. They are neither impersonal nor institutional. Caring times are recognised as prime times for developing a sense of well-being and personal worth and PRIME TIMES for learning. In the

process, each child derives a sense of individual importance and well-being.

(Greenman and Stonehouse 1996: 107)

These elements can be recognized in the 'peaceful caregiving as curriculum' approach implemented through 'primary caregiving' (Key Person Approach) by practitioners at the Childspace Ngaio Infants and Toddler Centre in New Zealand (Dalli and Kibble 2010), who were influenced by their study of Emmi Pikler and Magda Gerber's work (Petrie and Owen 2005). Through a process of action research, these practitioners identified the following key elements of their peaceful caregiving style:

- Language that describes and explains
- Hand and other bodily gestures
- Facial expressions and cooperative/ turn-taking behaviour.

(Dalli and Kibble 2010: 29)

An essential ingredient of these behaviours is being attuned to the child's responses and cues, such as movement and gestures as well as vocalizations. Different kinds of slow-paced gestures, such as gentle touch, affectionate touch and sensitive signalling touch were identified as a key way in which practitioners and children indicate their meaning to each other and when these cues are read correctly, such actions and language result in children's willing engagement in care activities (Dalli and Kibble 2010). This level of cooperation is characterized by the adult responding sensitively to the child's cues and thereby following the child's lead in setting the pace of the interaction. The practitioners identified a pattern of care they call ISE: Invite, Suggest, Engage (Dallie and Kibble 2010). Similarly, in the Key Times Action Research Project (Manning-Morton and Thorp 2006), practitioners at Hampden Children's Centre in London developed a protocol for physical care activities as follows:

When we interact physically with children we will:

- Invite the children
- Help the child to identify what needs doing
- Let the child know what we intend to do
- Be at their level
- Be calm and offer reassurance
- Follow the children's non-verbal communications
- Handle the children gently
- Make opportunities for the children to do things for themselves.

As the last point indicates, providing well for 2-year-olds during these times also means providing for their capacity for autonomy and independence and working collaboratively together with children to gain shared understandings in what Colwyn Trevarthen calls 'companionship' (Trevarthen and Aitken 2001; Trevarthen 2002).

Companionship

Trevarthen's concept of 'companionship', although aligned with Bowlby's concept of attachment, is also different. Trevarthen equates attachment with care and the kind of relationship in which a child's state of well-being or comfort is nurtured, while in companionship 'subjects act collaboratively with joint and mutually aware interest in their common world of objects and places where they may act and plan actions together, they gain intersubjective understanding of common meanings' (Trevarthen and Aitken 2001: 15). The emphasis here is more on mutuality and cooperation. This is the companionship that leads to confident confiding, to cultural learning and to language (Trevarthen and Aitken 2001; Trevarthen 2002).

As well as a collaborative psychological environment, the physical space should be organized for optimum independence, for example, in the bathroom, by arranging flannels, towels and toilet paper within children's reach, having steps up to the changing table so they can climb up themselves and taps that they can turn on and off. Also, labelling children's own things clearly means that they can identify and access them independently (Manning-Morton and Thorp 2006).

It is necessary to allow a lot of time for 2-year-olds to practise this kind of independence and also to engage happily in the kinds of learning and experimentation that bathroom and mealtimes offer. The Childspace Ngaio practitioners identified one of the unspoken rules that underpin their practice as 'This can take as long as it needs to take' so they did not pressurize each other to get through routines in specific time periods (Dalli and Kibble 2010: 31). Pressure to get through bathroom and mealtime routines quickly can sometimes also come from organizational structures such as the working hours of domestic support staff or practitioners' lunch breaks. These issues require those in leadership roles to support practitioners by changing any structural barriers to implementing positive care routines. This means they too need to understand and be clear about the importance of these care activities as a central focus of the curriculum.

Toilet learning

Case study

In the following observation Bianca (KP) records Bella's (2y5m) first day in pants.

'Bella, are you wearing knickers today?' I asked. 'Yes, I got pretty ones,' she said. I explained that she could use the toilet or a potty. 'I go toilet,' said Bella walking into the cubicle. Bella pulled her trousers down, and sat on the toilet. 'I finished,' said Bella standing up; she had not been to the toilet. 'I need potty.' I took a potty down from the shelf, putting it onto the bathroom floor. 'No, I want white one,' said Bella. I took down the white one. Bella stood behind the potty and bent down placing one hand on each side of the potty holding it still. Bella then moved her feet forwards to walk onto the potty but her trousers around her ankles stopped her from being able to get onto the potty.

'Would you like me to help you, Bella?' I enquired. 'No, I help myself, I do it,' Bella said then placed the potty behind her and sat down on the potty. She then stood up. 'I need toilet.' Bella then walked back into the cubicle and closed the door. She stood behind the door and shouted, 'I finished'. 'Bella, if you have finished, you need to pull your trousers up and wash your hands,' I suggested. 'No, no toilet, no potty,' she said pulling her trousers up and coming out of the cubicle. Bella looked up at me and smiled, 'I got knickers.' 'Yes, Bella, you're a big girl, if you need the toilet come and tell me or your pretty trousers will get all wet.'

Later that morning Bella stood by the toilet watching Mia go to the toilet. Suddenly she said, 'Bella don't like it, I wet, Bianca.' I looked down and noticed Bella's trousers were wet. 'It's OK, Bella, you have wet yourself that's why you need to use the toilet like Mia when you don't have a nappy on.'

I learned a lot from this about the continuity and support Bella needed. If it had been a different practitioner, they wouldn't have known the conversation we had had earlier. I'm glad that we have a Key Person Approach that ensures each Key Person takes their children to the bathroom.

A hugely important piece of learning for a 2-year-old is learning to use the toilet independently. Unfortunately it is still the case that in many homes and early childhood settings, children's toilet learning is treated as a process begun at a time deemed 'right' by the adults, often as a result of top-down pressure for children to be 'clean and dry' before they can start in a setting or move into an older age group. This approach disregards an individual child's readiness and does not adhere to the kind of respect for the child's bodily integrity emphasized by Pikler and Gerber (cited in Petrie and Owen 2005). Toilet learning is a useful example of the multi-faceted nature of children's development. Toddlers' readiness for using the potty or toilet is determined not only by their physical control but also by their social, emotional and intellectual understanding. When these influences coincide and they are supported by flexible routines and encouraging adults working in partnership, then they learn very quickly. If children are coerced into using the toilet or potty, their drive to be self-determining is likely to emerge through defiance and uncooperativeness. Through being helped to feel proud and in control, children are more likely to succeed in this area of learning.

Toilet learning is also an area fraught with differing personal and professional feelings and values so practitioners and parents need to discuss together how to plan this process. This should include issues such as naming and discussing body parts and products as families often have their own words for these things. Practitioners also need to reflect on their own personal reactions to bodily functions; young children are very interested in their bodies and its products, including things like playing with the mucus from their noses or the contents of their nappy/potty. These behaviours can provoke strong negative responses in adults, so it is important that practitioners keep the importance of children developing a positive self-concept uppermost in their minds and not let their own attitudes to food, bodily waste or dirt make a caring time negative for a child by, for example, using words like dirty or smelly (Greenman and Stonehouse 1996) or using negative body language or voice tone. The extent to which a child retains a sense of pride and pleasure in their physical self depends largely on whether the parent or practitioner responds to their natural curiosity with horror or calm matter-of-factness (Lieberman 1995; Manning-Morton 2006).

Smoothing the journey through the day

Practitioners often say that young children need routine as it helps them to feel secure when the flow of the day is familiar. For 2-year-olds, whose concepts of time are still developing, this can be very true. Regularity and predictability can be reassuring: they also allow them to practise important cognitive skills such as planning and predicting. However, 2-year-olds are also practising their newfound independence and autonomy and therefore can find conforming to group expectations a challenge or an opportunity to practise their skills in asserting their own choices and decisions. This means that practitioners need to structure the day so that adult-imposed changes in environment and activity are minimal and also build in plenty of time for making any necessary transitions such as between playing and eating or sleeping and waking, or being indoors and going out on a visit. Develop ways of alerting and preparing children for the change such as giving warnings and choices, such as 'When we have finished eating tea, it will be time to get ready to go home,' or 'Would you like to have some fruit before you paint or afterwards?' (Manning-Morton and Thorp 2006). It is also important to ensure that the message is delivered clearly. Sometimes in the hustle and bustle of a transition time, practitioners may all join in giving out instructions, resulting in either conflicting messages if they are not listening to each other or repeated demands with no time in between for a child to think, gather themselves together and begin to comply, resulting in feeling 'nagged' and therefore resentful. As 2-year-olds like to practise their autonomy, involving the children in these processes not only helps the practitioner but creates opportunities for children to feel competent and develop a sense of belonging and contribution (Ministry of Education 1996).

So, the regularity and predictability of routine need to be balanced with flexibility, as in Rima's response to Ollie in the case study. Although most 2-year-olds will gradually adapt to the setting's routine, at first it is their own individual routine that they need to follow and even when settled and 'at home' in the setting, if they are tired or hungry, they will not understand that lunch is not available for another half an hour or that they are expected to sleep after lunch (DfES Sure Start 2002). Having a rigid routine to the day does not consider that children have individual needs which both fluctuate daily and change over time.

Sleeptimes

Fluctuations in children's needs are particularly clear with 2-year-olds' need for rest and sleep. A just-2-year-old will usually have a need for more sleep than a nearly-3-year-old but a nearly-3-year-old who is having a growth spurt may revert to wanting a rest when a few weeks previously they had no need for one. Therefore there must be a balance between having familiar, predictable times of day and the flexibility to change times according to children's particular needs and growth patterns. This requires practitioners to be very observant of their key children's behaviours and to be in close and regular communication with their key children's parents/carers. Parents' circumstances and therefore their wishes regarding how much and when their children sleep during the day will vary. Some, whose children have a long day and perhaps a long journey home may want their child to sleep so that they can have some family time in the evening; for others, having a bouncy, demanding 2-year-old awake late into the evening may try their patience too far!

Reflective exercise

Think about the 2-year-olds in your care.

- What do you know about what each of their parents want and need to happen in relation either sleeping or toilet learning?
- How have you incorporated those wishes and needs into your practice?
- How have you resolved any differences of approach between you?

For practitioners, balancing the parents' needs and wishes with the immediate need for a child to sleep or not sleep can mean that the bridge they are building between home and setting feels a bit like a suspension bridge in a high wind! The key here is negotiation and compromise and constant communication in which all voices are heard, including the child's. It is not respectful of the child (even if possible) to forcefully keep them awake or make them sleep, but keeping their nap short or taken earlier, or ensuring there are enough quiet times during the day for children to have 'down time', may be a compromise for the adults, which won't compromise the child's bodily integrity too much.

The arrangements for sleep or rest are another aspect of being in this strange 'country' that new children may find bewildering, as Ollie did in the case study. Sleeping on mats or in sleeping bags on the floor may seem very strange, so having their parent/ carer there with them when they first stay at that time would help to give reassurance. Falling asleep in another's presence requires trust; when that person is unfamiliar, it is not a comfortable thing to do, so it is important that children have their Key Person with them, at least until they are very well settled and confident in the group and always when they are upset or unwell. Equally, waking up in a different place and with unfamiliar people is very disorientating and some people are slow to wake, others wake up quickly; such differing needs are to be respected and responded to sensitively. For example, with some children it is better to approach them more indirectly, quietly moving around the room rather than talking to them straight away, as they may take longer to adjust when they wake. Sleeping is like another separation for 2-year-olds. This may mean that they resist sleeping when they feel unsettled or insecure; they need their comfort object and familiar rituals to help them. It also means that the organization of staff breaks should be led by the children's needs. On the other hand, this is also a useful time to support a 2-year-old's growing independence. When sleep mats and blankets or sleeping bags and baskets for socks and shoes are always in the same place and accessible, it facilitates children getting themselves ready for a rest. As in all other aspects of practice with 2-year-olds, the skill of the practitioner is in being attuned to the child's need for both independence and comfort and closeness.

In settings that have 0–2-year-olds, arrangements for a suitable space for sleeping will be established but where settings have previously catered only for children over 3 years old, particularly schools, suitable arrangements for sleeping and eating will have to be developed. For sleeping, children need a consistent, separate area that is quiet and relaxed, with low lighting and soft furnishings and where children can access their own mat and blanket/ sleeping bag and not be disturbed by the other children.

Mealtimes

Similarly, mealtimes in provision focused on older children may be arranged in ways that are manageable for 3–5-year-olds but difficult for 2-year-olds. For example, having to move to a different (and often noisy) space with large groups of children and maybe different adults is the kind of situation that is likely to trigger overwhelming feelings of bewilderment and lack of control, leading to the stereotypical behaviours of an uncooperative, defiant, tantruming 2-year-old. Instead, mealtimes should be organized with children sitting in small groups with their Key Person and in a familiar, contained space. This kind of arrangement is more likely to result in the kind of relaxed, social and conversational event that we as adults value when eating out with friends or at home with our families. We may like the bustle and excitement of a large gathering at special occasions but would not choose to do this every day, so why do we expect children, whose senses are more acute and whose social skills less mature, to have to manage the demands that come from eating with large, noisy groups of people?

New children will need much support when being introduced to the culture and rituals of mealtimes in a nursery setting. For some, sitting at tables in a group for a prolonged length of time may be very different to the arrangements at home for such young children. Similarly, the type of food offered, how it is offered (mashed or whole) and how it is eaten (with fingers or implements) are experiences that are all potentially different and strange. Early childhood settings are usually keenly aware of providing a variety of healthy balanced meals such as those suggested by the Children's Food Trust in their guidelines (2012). Sometimes, however, the level of variety may be a challenge for some 2-year-olds who, as we have discussed, often like things to be familiar and predictable. This requires practitioners, parents and cooks to discuss how to provide maybe a smaller range of meals that are both nutritionally healthy and reflective of children's cultural backgrounds but will form a familiar base, to which new and different foods can be added as optional extras.

Mealtimes, like sleep times, are potential sites of conflict between adults and 2-year-olds as these are times when children will seek to assert their independence and autonomy and practise their abilities to make choices and decisions in the context of an adult-imposed agenda! So organizing for maximum independence is essential. For example, having suitable and sufficient bowls and serving spoons so children can serve themselves and small jugs with lids so they can pour their own drinks without spilling, gives children independence, while having the serving bowls on the table allows for excellent opportunities for the children to exercise a degree of choice regarding foods they like and for small or large helpings.

Gathering together to share food is universally a social time during which a sense of belonging and friendship is created. Sitting in small groups, as identified earlier, is important so 2-year-olds can make themselves heard and effective conversations can take place. Using place mats to organize and identify seating is useful but if children wish to sit next to a particular friend, then the flexibility to change seating arrangements must be in place. A mealtime can seem a long time to sit still for an active 2-year-old so it is a good idea to wait until the food is ready before asking the children to sit at the table and involving children in setting the table will occupy them and engage them in the process.

As with adults, some children will eat quickly, some more slowly, so practitioners need to ensure that they can remain sitting at the table with the children as much as possible so children have plenty of time to eat at their own pace. This can be helped by having the support of domestic staff to bring and clear away food and utensils and clean the area after the meal, as arranged by the settings involved in the Key Times Project in L.B. Camden (Manning-Morton and Thorp 2006).

Snack times

Two-year-olds are very active but only have small stomachs so they need to eat little and often. The Children's Food Trust suggests that children need to have two or three snacks daily in addition to three meals of breakfast, lunch and tea (2012). For children attending a setting for an extended day, this means that a lot of time is spent eating and drinking, therefore these times must be planned thoughtfully and balanced with 2-year-olds' need for uninterrupted play and exploration. Snack times are good opportunities for nurturing choice and autonomy, especially if a 'snack bar' arrangement is in place whereby a practitioner sits at a table where the snacks are available for a period of time (perhaps half an hour) and the children are invited to join when they are ready to take a break in their play. Alternatively, practitioners may decide to include having a snack during their key group time, where they are creating an 'Island of Intimacy' (Goldschmied and Jackson 2004) through having conversations about interesting objects or current interests and experiences.

Conclusion

From the examples of bathroom, sleep and meal times discussed in this chapter, it can be seen how vital the role of the Key Person is in providing consistency of experience through guiding and supporting their key children during their journey through the day and the setting. For children to have as consistent experiences as possible, for the times that the Key Person and child are together in the setting the Key Person should:

- Settle their key children as they arrive each day
- Eat with their key children in small key groups
- Change and toilet their key children
- Dress and wash their key children, offering help as needed but also supporting their growing skills.

Practitioners in group settings who have implemented this approach, consider the Key Person undertaking these tasks for 70 per cent of the time to be an achievable target. They ensure that for the remaining 30 per cent of the time the child's familiar secondary Key Person steps in (Manning-Morton and Thorp 2006). Practitioners who are new to working with this age group may prioritize other aspects of key working such as completing the children's 2-year check or planning play activities. While both of these things are important, if the Key Person Approach is to have any real meaning for 2-year-olds, it must be delivered through the concrete experiences of physical care, which require that practitioners pay good attention to this as a central aspect of their pedagogical approach (Goldschmied and Jackson 2004; Manning-Morton and Thorp 2003, 2006; Elfer et al. 2011). It is through planning and reflecting on physical care activities that 2-year-olds' positive self-concept can effectively be supported.

4 Meeting people: making friends, discovering diversity

Introduction

Previous chapters have discussed the importance of child/adult attachments for supporting children's emotional and personal development; this chapter focusses on how 2-year-olds' secure attachments with adults help them to form friendships and be part of a group. Becoming part of a wider social group such as a nursery for the first time entails meeting others who are different in many ways, so this chapter is also about how to foster a 2-year-old's sense of self and their interest and openness to difference.

Case studies

Lucy (2y9m) tends to be shy; she rarely speaks at the nursery but according to her parents talks at length at home. Her parents are English and Irish, and English is the sole language spoken at home. She is the older of two children and her brother Jamie is now in the younger group at nursery. She loves going to visit him, talking quietly to him as they play together. Her mother reports that, at home, Lucy sings all the nursery songs and talks in detail about the other children and what she has done during the day. She attends nursery full-time and was originally in the baby/toddler group. Now she is in a group of twenty children aged 2y6m to 4 years old.

* * *

Pascal (2y7m) is in the same group as Lucy. He started nursery two months previously and attends for 14 hours a week. He loves to be outside running, climbing and riding bikes. He mainly plays with one other child, Evo (2y7m). Pascal's home language is Greek and Evo's is Portuguese so their shared language is emergent English but they both love vigorous outdoor play. Pascal's mother reports that he is very attached to his older sister who is at secondary school and his grandmother who often comes to stay from Cyprus.

Meeting people and making friends

Reflective exercise

Take a few minutes to think about a close friend. Recall a time recently when you did something together – perhaps it was going on holiday or starting something new together? It could be playing a sport or shopping together for a forthcoming event. What did you value about this experience?

You may have noted that you valued the companionship, laughing together or the mutual sharing of ideas. Perhaps one of you inspired the other to try something new or you went to places you would never have gone alone. Maybe you mentioned the way you are able to 'read' each other's minds and know how to support each other when one of you is struggling. These recollections of the enjoyment of friendship lead us to consider the way 2-year-olds make friends and the way in which friendships can support and contribute to their sense of belonging and well-being.

Inexperienced practitioners may subscribe to the stereotypical view of 2-year-olds as being egocentric, unable to appreciate another's different point of view and unable to share and cooperate in a group; that is, that they are not very social beings at all! However, more recent writers and theorists and those working closely with this age group in settings where 2-year-olds' characteristics and development are understood, will refute this view. They will testify to the enormous interest most 2-year-olds have in others and in forming friendships (Trevarthen 2001; Dunn 2004). This can be clearly seen in the observation below, where Pascal and Evo also show elements of cooperative play in contrast to Parten's (1932) emphasis on 2-year-olds preferring solitary play or parallel play.

Pascal and Evo are in the garden. Pascal has taken a wooden spoon from the water play tray indoors. He is running up a little hill holding it above his head shouting, 'going on sark hun!' Evo watches him for a while, then, taking a shark from the water tray, follows him holding up the shark and shouting just like Pascal. Pascal lets Evo catch up with him. He says 'No,' takes the shark, runs back indoors and comes out with another spoon. He gives the spoon to Evo and they set off down the hill shouting, 'Sark hunt!' At the bottom of the hill Pascal says, 'Hide!' and they both dive into the bushes.

Interestingly whilst theirs is an established friendship, in this scenario Evo follows the pattern usually taken by young children as they initiate a new friendship. First, a toddler or 2-year-old will watch with interest, then imitate the other child, then add another feature to the imitation. If the overture to be friends is accepted, this gets adopted by the new friend who then transforms it again into something new. In this way, young children's friendships tend to be formed around common interests (Manning-Morton and Thorp 2003, 2006). The rich, mutually rewarding play with close friends, as seen in the case study, is characterized by the contribution of new ideas by each child and is 'emotionally absorbing, and exciting' for those playing (Dunn 2004: 1): First Evo accepts Pascal's direction for their play then he takes the lead; they are totally enthralled by their 'escaping the shark' game.

Practitioners working with this age group will notice that attachments between young children are clearly made but the desire for exclusivity is yet to become as important as it is for older children's friendships (Dunn 2004). Some 2-year-olds may not form particular friendships but still thrive as part of a circle of friends. This is equally an arena in which self-identity and the ability to understand and respond to the feelings of others can flourish. However, if potential friends are to really get to know each other and enjoy the companionship identified in the reflective exercise above, children need to have consistent contact over time for their friendships to develop and become established (Howes and James, cited in Smith and Hart 2011), so the constancy of children's peer groups is crucial. One of the drawbacks of the current 2-year-old funding policy (DFE 2011) in the UK is that many 2-year-olds are in part-time places, so the population of any group may change daily, thereby interfering with the process of establishing satisfying and rewarding friendships.

Factors such as these that are present in the macrosystem (Bronfenbrenner 1979) can then be seen to impact on all aspects of children's development because all aspects of development and learning are closely intertwined. For example, the process of thinking and talking about emotions in social relationships includes the kind of reflective, problem-solving processes that are fundamental to cognitive understanding. In turn, the emergence of language also contributes to making friends; ideas can be shared as with Evo's 'Hide!' so making contact, following and imitating is more possible now.

Young children's friendships then, particularly when they involve pretend play, are a key way in which they develop and hone their social skills. Although they can practise social skills when participating in collaborative thinking with adults, play with peers requires more adaptation to the perspectives of less socially skilled play partners (Rogoff 1990). In this way, rich pretend play with other children is largely dependent on the development of theory of mind (TOM) and empathy. Evo needs to have thought about

Pascal's interests, recognized how they are like his own and adapted his behaviour to make social contact with him.

Theory of mind or mind sight and mirror neurons

Theory of mind is the ability to understand that other people may hold different viewpoints, desires, wishes and motivations to you. Although you cannot know for certain what the other person is thinking, you infer this from your understanding of their actions and behaviours and from your understanding of your own feelings, desires and motivations and from your experience of being in a similar situation. From this you develop a 'theory' about the other person's state of mind.

Research that has used 'false belief' structured tests to explore this shows that 2–3–year-olds have yet to develop theory of mind (Gopnik and Wellman 1994, cited in Berk 2009). However, researchers such as Judy Dunn (2004), who study children in their social context rather than through a structured test, suggest that the ability to perceive that others may have a different perspective and think and feel differently from them is evident in younger children. She describes theory of mind as 'mind reading' (2004) and cites examples of this being apparent in family life, drawing on observations of 15- to 23-month-olds teasing siblings by running off with their special toy, for example, thereby showing that they understand another's feelings and wishes (Dunn 2004).

In neuroscience, mirror neurons in the brain have been taken to be the mechanism by which we understand others. A mirror neuron is a neuron which fires both when we perform an action and when we observe the same action performed by another. So, the different functions of the mirror neuron system include understanding intentions, theory of mind and empathy. The basic system for this is thought to be present in newborn infants but matures according to experience (Viraj-Babul et al. 2012).

From an alternative perspective, Siegel calls the capacity to perceive the mind of the self and others 'mindsight' (1999: 149). He links this to security of attachment, identifying that where parents/carers do not focus on the mental states of the child or where their own mental states are intrusive on the child's, the acquisition of theory of mind is impaired (Siegel 1999).

Showing concern for others

Empathy is closely connected to theory of mind, as it also requires the child to have a sense of self: that is, to see themselves as distinct from others

(Schaffer 2006). By the age of 2, many children are able understand what another might be feeling and to make some good judgements about what might make them feel better. Those working with 2-year-olds will be familiar with their use of phrases such as "He wants his Mummy", or "Danny doesn't like it!", which show empathy with feelings and also understanding of others' desires.

Case study

When Lucy arrived at nursery in the morning she saw that Pascal was crying by the door. She went up to him and in a soft, gentle voice said, "Mummy coming back soon, Pascal." Pascal nodded. She went to the garden door. Evo was on the slide outside. Lucy said, "Come out, Pascal."

Actually, Pascal had just hurt himself and he was waiting for his Key Person who had gone to fetch a plaster. But Lucy used her own experience and her understanding of what makes Pascal happy very skilfully here. Her development in this area may have been particularly encouraged as her parents are social workers and very used to tuning into Lucy's feelings. Such context is important as the ability to mind read is not innate. Rather it depends on the quality of the primary attachment relationship, the child's wider social experience and the parenting style adopted in their family (Shaffer 2006). Dunn et al. (1991) propose that children whose families frequently talk about emotions and each other's mental states are more able to understand the names of these different states and that different people can feel differently about the same thing (Dunn et al. 1991). Lucy's gender may also put her at an advantage here, as Dunn (1988) also notes that mothers talk about feelings more with their daughters than with their sons, which, it is suggested, results in the apparently more mature ability of girls to regulate feelings by the age of 8 (Malatesta and Haviland 1982, cited in Saarni 1984).

Empathy

Berk (2012: 415) defines empathy as: 'The ability to detect different emotions, to take another's emotional perspective, and to feel with that person, or respond emotionally in a similar way.' Hoffman (1988) identified a developmental progression in children's ability to empathize, which begins with what he called 'global empathy', for example, a baby cries when hearing others cry. This progresses to 'egocentric empathy' by 18 months when toddlers tend not only to respond to another's distress but attempt to alleviate it in the way that they would find most soothing, so they might offer their comfort blanket, for example. Then gradually from toddlerhood and throughout early school years children become increasingly skilled at detecting others' feelings and partially matching them using the immediate context.

Finally from late childhood onwards they progress to 'empathy for another's life condition' whereby children recognize that the sadness of the other person may not be related to immediate circumstances, but an ongoing feeling associated with a certain event or circumstance (Hoffman 1988).

Supporting 2-year-olds' emotional and social development

So a child draws on the experience and relationships that they have had from birth to gain what Goleman (1996) terms emotional intelligence. The ability to understand and differentiate emotions enables children to become more socially competent, as such emotional and relational knowledge and experience are then utilized in developing friendships. Therefore, by supporting the 2-year-old's emotional development we are enabling them to form helpful structures in their minds that allow them to be confident travellers in the wider world. This is particularly the case when working with 2-year-olds who may have experienced difficult circumstances before coming into the setting, which may put them at a social disadvantage. Dowling (2005: 68) suggests that 'the setting can play a crucial role in working with parents sharing the task of helping children understand what they feel'.

Reflective exercise

Monitor the expression of emotion and the conversations about emotional states between adults and children throughout one day. Note how often feelings are expressed and how others respond to these. Note if and how emotional states are talked about and with whom.

Your notes may reveal that there are merely functional references to emotions, for example, a practitioner saying, 'I'm not happy with the way you . . .' or, 'Look at his face! Is he happy with you?' You may have observed tokenistic discussion of feelings such as at circle times when children are asked to go round each saying how they feel. This is meaningless to a 2-year-old (and most children). To make sense of talk about feelings, any discussion must be embedded in a meaningful context such as in the example below.

Case study

Lucy, her Co-Key Person Kim and three other 2-year-olds are sitting together. Lucy is even quieter than usual. She looks worried. Kim notices Lucy's expression and says, 'This is different today for you isn't it, Lucy?' Lucy doesn't react. 'You are usually in Sara's group but Sara's not here today, is she? Do you feel a bit sad? Are you worried about who will take care of you?' Lucy looks at Kim. 'Sara hurt her ankle in the garden, didn't she? She is staying at home today. Poor Sara, I wonder if she has got a sad face too. I am going to look after you all day until tea time. Then Harry will have tea with you and stay with you until Daddy comes. Do you think you will be OK with that?' Lucy does not respond, eyes down.

Kim asks the others, 'What can we do to help Lucy feel better?' 'Tickle her!' suggests Hamza. 'That might work, Hamza, you like being tickled, don't you? Ask her first though.' Hamza says, 'Do you want tickle, tickle, tickle?' Lucy shakes her head. Faustina (2y11m) stands up and peels Sara's photo off the photo board and hands it to Lucy. Lucy takes it and holds it to her tummy. 'Wow, that's a good idea Faustina,' Kim says, 'Is that a bit better?' Lucy gives a little nod. 'Will you be Lucy's friend today, Faustina?' 'She can sit with me for dinner,' Faustina replies.

This kind of discussion helps children perceive, predict and respond to the feelings of others. It includes the genuine expression and recognition of emotional states. The practitioner models genuine concern, attuned 'mindsight' and provides words for the feelings perceived. She invites the other children to engage in Lucy's state of mind and to be empathetic; she affirms the children's attempts to do this and shows respect for Lucy by ensuring that she is able to reject or accept their offers of sympathy. One of the dangers of being a 'professional' (in the stereotypical sense) early years practitioner, is of carers not being real about their feelings or representing them inaccurately which makes it 'much more difficult for the child to express feelings and to negotiate around feelings with others' (Gerhardt 2004: 51). This can include practitioners adopting false brightness, fake enthusiasm or disapproval, pretending to feel hurt or cross, for example.

An issue to consider in the approach in the observation though, is that this kind of situation may result in some young 2-year-olds, or those with additional difficulties, getting distressed themselves rather than being able to offer sympathy to the upset child (Berk 2012), as other people's expressions of unhappiness may trigger feelings of anxiety and therefore negative behaviours. This example of practice though, took place in what this setting calls 'Island Time', which helps with this difficulty. The setting has a very effective Key Person system and before lunch every day each Key Person gathers their key children together for some small group time. Each key group has their special place to meet and that place also has a low level photographic display of the children in that key group and their Key Person. The anxiety felt by young children in what can be an emotional fairground in a large group, can be greatly helped by regular small group times such as these. They foster both the child's attachment to the Key Person and their close relationships with their peers. They provide opportunities for a sense of security and belonging to grow, and feelings to be expressed. This is where empathy can develop into helpful rather than destructive responses to others. These small groups can include action song times, quieter times for chatting as in the observation above or sharing a book or photo album. This idea was conceived by Elinor Goldschmied who called the small groups 'Islands of Intimacy' (Goldschmied and Jackson 2004: 46). She suggests using collections of special treasures which children can explore together, chatting as they play. These can be purses, torches or anything that might link to the interests of group members.

From this it is clear how the size of groups that 2-year-olds are in affect the quality of their play and ability to engage in pro-social behaviour (Harms et al. 1990). They need to have opportunities to be alone or to feel noticed and special in one-to-one or small groups, not constantly be part of a crowd. So, as well as organizing times for small key groups as in the observation above, settings need to consider the size of the peer group that 2-year-olds are in everyday, they should not have to be part of a large group for prolonged periods of time. If practitioners reflect on how stressful and tiring it can be to be part of a large group on a training session, for example, they will appreciate how, being 2 years old and with far fewer sophisticated social skills, being in such a situation may lead to the kind of negative behaviours often attributed to 2-year-olds.

Meeting people: discovering diversity

As discussed in Chapter 1, 2-year-olds are forming their self-concept and understanding of others through their close relationships with their primary carers but also with their siblings and Key Person. They are discovering answers to questions such as: Who am I? What can I do? Where do I belong? What do others think of me? Equally, they are asking, who are you? How are we the same or different? As they enter the wider social world of an early years setting, these questions will be answered in myriad ways through the practice and provision they experience. Whether the answers they receive are positive or negative will depend largely on whether practitioners show that they value the children's home cultures and the degree to which they reflect on and amend their attitudes and behaviours towards difference.

By 2 years of age children are aware of their gender in that they know if they are boys or girls and can make that distinction between others. However, they rely on visual cues to make these judgements and as these cues are culturally determined, this can let them down. For example, Lucy has very short hair and seldom wears skirts or dresses. At snack time Saffron, another 2-year-old at her nursery, asks, 'Why you let him get more grapes?' Hair, clothes and jewellery can confuse a 2-year-old who has yet to encounter boys who wear earrings or men who wear dhotis or sarongs. Moreover, they have yet to learn that people's gender usually does not change over time and boys will become men and girls women.

As well as gender, skin, eye and hair colour are part of each child's self-identity. Two-year-olds understand how these are valued through the significance they attribute to what and how adults talk about these things and, very importantly, to those things nobody mentions (but probably exude a sense of discomfort about). At the same time, a 2-year-old's interest in classification means they will be learning huge amounts about colours, shapes and how objects (and people) can be classified into groups. As they learn from the attitudes of those around them towards different groups, they may adopt these, classifying boys as leaders, girls as chatty or disabled children as less skilled, for example. What is significant is that such young children are not yet able to resist or refute the impressions they are forming (Abbot and Langston 2005); however, practitioners are in a very good position to introduce positive messages about diversity as in the example below.

Case study

Alannah (2y1m) often talks about Alicia (2y6m) who has cerebral palsy and uses a special chair and an iPad. When Alannah mentions Alicia, she rocks as she sees Alicia do; the name and action both identify who she is talking about. Her mother thinks her friendship with Alicia was initiated by Alannah's interest in both Alicia's special chair and her iPad. When Alicia is not using it, Alannah likes to climb into the chair and to adopt the same position Alicia uses. They enjoy looking at the iPad together and take turns to show each other the different effects they can create by pressing the screen. Alannah brings things in to show Alicia. She speaks about her a lot at home and when her mother collects Alannah from nursery she tells her, 'Alicia, Alicia' – normally she has already been collected so it is as if she is letting her Mum know who she has been playing with or that she is not there any longer. Her Key Person said that Alannah often goes to Alicia and tickles her on her neck which Alicia giggles at. As Alicia also has a visual impairment and limited language, the Key Person has been encouraging these spontaneous sensory experiences.

Here we do not see a child mocking another by their imitation but one who is genuinely interested in and keen to explore the different way of being she has encountered in meeting Alicia. However, some children may seem fearful of those who appear very different from themselves or people they are used to. A practitioner can help with this, first, by ensuring that this child's own sense of self is being affirmed; second, by commenting on what the children and adults in the group have in common (such as Alannah and Alicia's liking of the iPad) and then affirming differences in a clear, matter-of-fact way. This will enable children to grow comfortable with the knowledge that we all have differences and similarities and that this is interesting rather than something to fear or feel awkward about. Children will be better able to talk about these things if practitioners provide a supportive environment and the vocabulary to discuss and explore these ideas (Manning-Morton and Thorp 2006).

Sometimes children make hurtful remarks or laugh at others' differences. Whilst the temptation may be to ignore or justify these as unintentional and not meant to offend, it is important to correct the negative comment in the presence of both children in a way that unpicks the comment and offers an alternative response (Derman-Sparks and Olsen Edwards 2010). Manning-Morton and Thorp (2006: 113) give one example of an English 2-year-old saying, 'Your name is funny' to Yong, a Korean boy. The practitioner could respond, 'It's not a funny name, it's a nice Korean name. Does it sound funny because you have never heard it before? It might make Yong sad when you say that. Just tell Yong: "I don't know that name". Now you know a new name! Let's tell Yong your name.'

Brown (2001) advocates using Persona Dolls to combat discrimination and support children's explorations of and promotion of positive attitudes to difference. The dolls' names, birth dates, families, likes, dislikes, etc. remain constant. Like the children in the group, they have life experiences which unfold as they are used in story and discussion times. Each doll has a particular ethnic, cultural and physical identity, and family make-up. The dolls can be used to re-enact children's experiences and to reflect on the choices everyone has to act kindly or in hurtful ways.

Practitioners' ability to pass on positive messages about diversity is underpinned by how well they know (and value) the child's family and socio-cultural context. What the Key Person needs to know is the sort of information that they can weave into play and routines times throughout the day. For example, Evo's Key Person suggested they made a flea collar for the toy cat just like Magnus (Evo's cat) has just been given.

Other ways of introducing children to diversity, especially in settings where there are fewer socio-cultural differences, are to share one's own experiences of being a child. For example, when playing in the garden, Harrison made a hammock with the children and explained that when he was little, this is how he took his nap. Personal stories such as this – and, of course books – open children's minds to other worlds and experiences but these are most effective when related to a 2-year-old's immediate experience. For example, Miller (1990) suggests telling 'Wonderful Stories'. These begin 'There once was a wonderful group called [name of the group] where there were lots of wonderful children. One wonderful child was called Ade who had black, short, curly hair and liked to wear his Thomas the Tank Engine tee-shirt. There was wonderful . . . [the story continues naming and describing a couple of attributes of each child]. One day they . . . [then add experiences or events of that morning].' This celebrates diversity and aids language skills for talking about what they think and can recall. It is fun and allows children to include what they remember about the occasion.

It is common practice to promote diversity by including items from different cultures in settings. However, these need to be meaningful to a 2-year-old. They need to be familiar and of interest to the current children in the group rather than tokens. Having a dog basket in the home corner and empty packets of dog food, a lead and toy dog will be more relevant to Lucy who has two dogs at home than an Irish flag would. Parents may be willing to contribute relevant items if the concept and the practitioners' aims are explained. Recipes, music and stories are often asked for but items that are connected with parents' jobs or interests will also help to reflect and value the child's background, like disused disposable cameras for the child whose parent is a photographer, for example.

Many settings are conscious of the need to make a setting inviting and one that reflects diversity and includes community languages. Having photographic displays of the practitioners and children in each group can be a great talking point for children and parents. This is especially important for very young children as they may mispronounce the names of the adults and children in the nursery and, in large settings, parents may get confused as to who is who. Displays of photographs of the children, their friends and family at the children's height in their group room will further create a bridge between home and nursery and affirm and value each child's family. Using protective film means that they can be poked and prodded and kissed without being destroyed.

All of these strategies can support 2-year-olds' understanding and acceptance of diversity but the most influential of them all is the practitioner's own attitudes and how these are conveyed to the children.

Conclusion

The 2-year-old's ability to make friends, engage in rich, creative pretend play and to understand and relate well to others is strengthened by everything the setting does to create a sense of belonging for each child in the group and between every child and adult. Rather than attributing a child's social difficulties to their age only, practitioners need to consider a range of factors. These include the 2-year-old's previous experience of being with peers, the amount of language a child has, how well the children know each other, the size of the group, how constant the group is, how the child is feeling physically or emotionally, the quality of their relationships with adults and the encouragement to talk about feelings and be interested in others' differences. In fact these are just the same factors that influence our ability to be sociable as adults! The role of the practitioner is to be sensitive to the children as individuals and to try to understand which factors are influencing each child's ability to make and sustain friendships.

5   Making myself understood: communicating with others

Introduction

When we travel to new lands, we need to be able to communicate with the people we encounter and then relate our experiences to those back at home. This can be taxing even for adults (especially if monolingual), so imagine how challenging it is when you are only 2 years old and your spoken language is often misunderstood by people who do not know you well. For this reason, this chapter focuses on how 2-year-olds make themselves understood in a range of ways, verbally and non-verbally. It discusses the strategies practitioners can adopt to support the communications of 2-year-olds learning one or more languages and considers the ways in which 2-year-olds understand the communications of others.

> **Case study**
>
> Nina (2y2m) is eating her breakfast and her mum (Rachel) is washing up. They are chatting about the visit to Nina's new nursery that morning.
>
> N: Gaggy coming?
> R: No just us, Pumpkin and me. And we will see Jenna [Nina's Key Person] there. She came to our house, didn't she?
> N: (laughs) Abba [her father] coming?
> R: No just us, Pumpkin and me.
> L: Scuff coming?
> R: No just us, Pumpkin and me. Have you finished your breakfast yet?
> N: I do three more spoons
>
> At this point Rachel breaks off to answer the phone. A protracted discussion ensues to convince the boiler repair man to return without charge as his repairs were ineffective.

Giggling Nina asks: Bekfast coming?
R: No just us, Pumpkin and me. Your breakfast would have to grow some legs to come with us. Better just finish it here. Not Gaggy, not Abba, not Scruff, not breakfast, just us.
N: And Special [the photo album about nursery left by Jenna at their home visit] come too.
R: Oh good girl! I nearly forgot, we've got to take that back, haven't we?

In the short vignette above we see Nina's mother, Rachel, using language to interact playfully with her daughter. She creates a warm emotional environment, prepares her for what is happening that day and reminds her of past experiences that would put the day's activity in context. Alongside this she succinctly describes a problem, clearly states what she wants and responds to unsatisfactory excuses in her conversation with the boiler man. Rachel's ability to be articulate makes her more able to get her needs met, maintain contact with others, express her thinking, be in control, give and gain information and create imaginary worlds. These are described by Halliday (1975) as the seven functions of talk. Moreover, Rachel is laying a foundation in Nina's mind that communication with others is rewarding, helping Nina to become a competent, confident communicator – what a valuable gift!

Reflective exercise

Look back at Nina's part in this conversation. What elements of Halliday's seven functions of talk has she gained in just two years? Think about recent conversations that you have had. How well were you able to employ these functions? Do some functions of talk come more easily than others?

Most children become fluent in their home language by 5 years old but the functional level of language and enjoyment of communicating that we see above begin in infancy. Bruner (1977) believed that the basic schemas for developing language are present very early in life and that early social games and interactions between carer and baby help babies to grasp the turn-taking form of conversation and that this is a rich means of giving and receiving information (Bruner 1977).

However, a new phase of Nina's life is about to begin. She is about to be placed in a new forum in which to communicate. Nina, along with many other 2-year-olds in the UK, is about to start at an early years setting. This is a place where none of her familiar adults, who know her story, will be present. They do not know that Gaggy is her grandmother, Scruff is the dog, or that Abba is her father. They don't know that 'three more spoonfuls' is said towards the end of every meal and that the empty plate is then clapped. This is Nina's language world and she is about to encounter a new world with only short sentences in her spoken repertoire with which to explain herself and to tell her story.

We are social beings and, in order to feel comfortable, need to explore how we fit together and into the social systems in which we find ourselves. So enabling 2-year-olds to tell their story, to get to know others' stories and how this new social group works is a central concern of early years practice. What follows is a discussion of key elements that will enable this to happen, that is:

- Listening to 2-year-olds
- Knowledge and understanding of the paths language and communication can take
- Detailed knowledge of each child
- Creating a rich language environment.

Listening to 2-year-olds' communications

Because their spoken language is still emerging, 2-year-olds rely heavily on communicating in multi-faceted ways. Understanding this and careful listening enable practitioners to have more mutually rewarding conversations with young children than those who rely solely on the spoken word. This may seem obvious; in fact all human communications are mostly non-verbal. But by analysing the following scenario, it becomes clear how the intricacy of 2-year-olds' communications, which require close attention to detail, can be a challenge for practitioners.

Case study

A group of twelve 2-year-olds and three practitioners are playing in different places around their group room. One practitioner is seated on the floor and children are bringing her differently coloured and shaped blocks from a construction area. She is pleased to receive each one saying to each: 'Ooh, what's this?' The presenting children reply, some naming the shape, some the colour, one says the circles are pancakes, some just smile. The practitioner is delighted with each reply. As the play progresses the children seem to be imitating each other, those previously using colour names now using shape names, or making the shape represent food. One child is watching this play. He seems less confident, perhaps about gaining a turn amongst this exuberant group or perhaps because this is not his Key Person.

A little later when the other children's play has moved on to something else, he gathers about five of the shaped blocks and presents them to another practitioner, with a smile and expectant look. The busy practitioner asks the child to put them in the construction area where they belong. The 2-year-old just stands there holding them out. Some remonstrating follows and eventually the child puts them back.

In the first part of this observation, we see how being available, at the child's level, and open to whatever the 2-year-olds want to communicate, allows ideas and conversation to flow.

Reflective exercise

What can you identify that children are learning in the first part of the observation? What is the practitioner doing that is enabling this? Identify the fine detail.

You may have noted that the practitioner is learning about each child's interests, their understanding of shape and colour names and their interest in representing their experiences. In addition, a lot of social and emotional learning is taking place as the children also learn from each other. But a lot of this is less obvious; for example, the children are also learning that this person is interested, values what they do and who they are. The children understand this mostly through the practitioner's body language, position, gestures, facial expressions and her voice tone. Practitioners use the same cues to understand children but it is easy to miss vital clues in a busy environment. In the second part of the observation, had the child said, 'I've got a present for you!' the practitioner might have responded with the same delight as the first practitioner. But for this child, his facial expression and body language had to be 'listened to' more attentively for this to be understood.

Another feature that can hinder a child being heard is stuttering. Two-year-olds often struggle to get their sentences out, especially if under pressure. For example, they may start a sentence, 'I go, I go . . .' a number of times. Goldschmied suggests quieting the other children then gently holding the hand of the struggling child, which seems to relax them and enable speech to flow (Goldschmied and Jackson 2004).

The kind of active listening referred to here is encapsulated by the National Children's Bureau Young Children's Voices Network (Clark 2009) which defines listening as an active process of receiving, interpreting and responding to communication using all the senses and emotions and not limited to the spoken word. Listening, they assert, underpins effective practice as it enables young children's feelings, needs, ideas and opinions to be understood but should also be an 'on-going part of tuning in to all children as individuals in their everyday lives' (Clark 2009: 1). Moreover, it is important that this 'listening' uses a range of tools so that all children are included, particularly the youngest children, those learning more than one language and those with a learning difficulty or physical disability. Furthermore, it benefits practitioners and settings as they reflect on and evaluate their practice and provision in response to sharing the children's perspectives.

Understanding the paths of communication and language development

Notwithstanding the importance of non-verbal expression in 2-year-olds' communications, the third year of life also sees children's language skills growing in both receptive and expressive language. At 2, a child's level of receptive language should not be underestimated as it far exceeds that which a child can express. Understanding is drawn from both the words and the 'tune' of the language young children hear. From birth infants listen more intently to human speech over other sounds and hear a string of sounds when listening to conversation. Young babies are especially attentive to Child Directed Speech (CDS) which has higher vocal sounds with slow short sentences, pronounced intonation and stressed words; moreover, CDS has been found to aid later word recognition (Soderstrom, cited in Brook and Kempe 2014). By the age of 2 these enthusiastic language learners have become increasingly competent, dividing what they hear into little units (Berk 2009). A similar process takes place when adults learn to understand a new language; for example, new speakers of French might hear the tune of 'Avez-vous choisi?' without really understanding that these are three separate words, they just know it is the cue to order their meal.

The 'tune' also includes intonation, the emphasis put on certain words in a sentence, which can have a profound effect on the meaning. For example, saying the same few words 'come and sit down' in a kindly, inviting way sounds very different to when said in an exasperated way. This use of emphasis is to convey meaning, but also it is influenced by the speaker's emotions. Trevarthen and Aitken (1994) argue that the emotional tune of communication conveys a stronger message than the words and it is this message to which 2-year-olds' brains are particularly sensitive. This is borne out by practitioners who have unintentionally snapped at a child and seen them close down emotionally and socially or become truculent over a simple, well-meant request such as to join the others for a snack. This way of using emphasis to convey meaning is quickly adopted by 2-year olds who may say, '*meee* do it!' if impatient to be independent or say quietly, 'me do it?' with a rising intonation, if wanting to check if they are capable or allowed.

The conventions of different languages, dialects and accents also dictate the 'tune'. A 2-year-old entering an early years setting in the UK may find the sound of English a disconcerting contrast to the sound of their home language. Or the English of their Londoner Key Person may be difficult to understand by the Liverpudlian 2-year-old. It takes time and effort on both parts to tune in and to understand each other. This is also true of practitioners and parents, where the intonation used in their first language may register a different tune to that which is expected or intended in English.

In the third year of life, expressive language is usually really taking off. Two particular features of 2-year-olds' language are the child echoing the last few words at the end of a sentence they hear, and the use of short sentences or telegraphic speech (Berk 2009) that they create themselves, as Nina does in the case study ('Scruff coming?'). These sentences soon become longer and some understanding of grammar will be apparent, often through the child's errors: 'I runned to shop'. Certain phonemes will be difficult for a 2-year-old to pronounce for example, s, ch, sh, z, j, v, and th and some ends of words may be missing (Rathus and Facaro 1988) as Nina showed by using 'an' instead of 'and'.

Language and communication: a social, emotional and intellectual travel ticket

Any difficulty a 2-year-old has with pronunciation is usually more than compensated for by the ingenious ways they use to express themselves. Declarative pointing will usually have been joined by 'what's that?' questions. These are used to build vocabulary and aid the 2-year-old's understanding of the world. They are also very useful ways to engage an adult's attention or even to distract the adult in much the same way an adult thinks that they can distract the cross or upset 2-year-old. A childminder recounted the following:

> **Case study**
>
> Hannah (2y0m) often points and says, 'What that?' both to get our attention and to delay something. The other afternoon I said, 'Hannah, time to brush your teeth.' This produced a 'No bed!' then a series of 'What that?' questions to delay what she knew teeth brushing was leading to.

This example demonstrates how developing language is essentially about social communication. Duffy et al. (2006) remind us that young children learn to say little etiquette scripts, prompted by their parents to produce them for certain occasions, for example, on the arrival of a visitor or before eating. These spoken scripts join the already understood gestures that are specific to that family's culture. Whilst a 2-year-old entering a setting will gain from learning how these vary across cultures, to feel understood themselves, their own scripts need to be known. For example, in the case study of Leyla, Jenna quickly learnt what 'three more spoons meant'. Those regularly talking to 2- to 3-year-olds will be familiar with the difficulty of following a 'story' the child might want to tell. Knowledge of context will give both child and practitioner a mutually rewarding end to their dialogue.

There is also a strong link between language and the 2-year-old's emotional memory and the need to express this repeatedly, as in the example below:

> **Case study**
>
> Parking outside the post office triggers Billie's (2y0m) memory of an event many months ago when she was lifted out of her car seat and set down on the pavement. She inadvertently stepped back on a large pile of dog mess. She wants to talk about this time and time again. She says, 'Disgussin, disgussin. Shoes all gone.' I then have to recount the story and she adds, 'Shoes in bin' because I threw the poo-caked shoes away.

Repetition such as Billie is engaging in is an important feature of language development as it helps the 2-year-old's cognitive understanding of an experience too. The ability to think is integral to language and communication skills but exactly how this happens has historically been the subject of much debate. A Vygotskian perspective suggests that language shapes thinking

(Vygotsky 1986) whereas in a Piagetian perspective (Piaget 1959), the ability to think shapes the ability to talk. For example, Jacy (2y9m) is out by the pegs putting his boots on. He is quietly talking to himself. He says, 'Oh no, wrong foot!' Swapping to the other foot he adds, 'Push, push, stand up.' Piaget viewed these monologues or 'egocentric' speech (Piaget 1959) as evidence of a pre-operational child's immaturity. However, Vygotsky described this as 'private speech' used to plan actions when problem solving. Conversation with others, however, is probably the most well-noted feature of the interrelationship of thought and language through which children and adults 'jointly construct meaning' (Robson 2006: 117). Although a 2-year-old will still be largely exploring the world through physical means, they are rapidly adding the tools of language to aid their explorations. By the end of their third year, children may be asking 'why' questions and be showing a greater ability to speculate about the future and to talk about past events more specifically so that the listener is less reliant on knowing the context.

Journeying in more than one language

Children who are making this journey with more than one language used to be seen as disadvantaged, but now growing up fluent in more than one language is widely recognized as a cognitive advantage. This is because it enables more creative thinking, as those with additional languages become aware of the abstract nature of language much earlier than mono-linguists (Mukerji and O'Dea 2000; Siraj-Blatchford and Clarke 2000). In addition, the National Literacy Trust report (2014) cites research by Yoshida (2008) that links bilingualism to increased levels of self-control, as well as emphasizing the useful way in which a bilingual child transfers knowledge and ideas between languages, thereby enhancing their cognitive understanding.

A 2-year-old may become bi- or multi-lingual in one of two ways: either simultaneously, when two or more languages are being learned together, or successively when, for example, a first language is established at home and the second acquired when entering an early years setting or moving to a different country. Simultaneous language learners at 2 will follow the same path as monolingual learners (Siraj-Blatchford and Clarke 2000). One parent reported that her daughter uses certain phrases or single words in each language and changes between English and Portuguese; sometimes her daughter stops using a word she knows in one language and starts to use the new word she has learnt for the same thing from the other language. This is not evidence of confusion that will result in language delay; rather it is a natural developmental stage of bilingualism. What is evident is the early ability of children to code switch, even before 2 years old. For example, outside the nursery 20-month-old Chia was heard to ask her father, '¿Qué es eso?' pointing at a stone pigeon in the car park. A short time later, seated on her Key Person's knee looking at a book, she pointed to a picture and asked, 'What's that?'

Although known to be a cognitive advantage, some practitioners think that the social and emotional well-being of children in early years settings who are learning English as an additional language is compromised (Manning-Morton 2014). This may be as a result of practitioners not fully understanding patterns of language development. Whitehead (2010: 38) gives the example of the 'bucket myth' whereby the brain is thought of as a container that can only hold a certain amount of language so learning two or more will be at the detriment of fully learning one language. Some may cite the example of successive language learners who may appear slow to talk, whereas what they are actually going through is a silent period of watching and listening not only to the new vocabulary but also to the new sets of sounds and intonations they are hearing (Clarke 1992). Overall these children follow similar patterns to all language learners as will children who are bi-lingual in signed languages. Any adverse impact on children's well-being might be because the setting has not given adequate attention to creating an inclusive environment. This applies to children whose language expression or learning is affected by a learning difficulty or physical disability too.

The use of signing is a key strategy in addressing this issue. As well as signing systems such as Makaton, a 2-year-old may have unique signs within their family. Parents may have been using baby signing to help their young child to communicate their needs and lessen their frustration. Children with hearing difficulties may have been communicating through signing as may those for whom autism is a possible facet of their development (Mukerji and O'Dea 2000). Specialist help in providing an effective communication environment tuned to a particular child's needs will assist practitioners; this may be from the child's main carers or agencies that are supporting the family. For example, gaining the advice of a speech and language therapist alerted one setting to how to reduce background noise to make the environment more conducive to a child with a cochlear implant.

A 2-year-old may also gain great benefit from using signing if their difficulty is in controlling or coordinating lip and tongue movements, which make it hard to pronounce or to sequence certain sounds and therefore difficult to make themselves understood (Mukerji and O'Dea 2000). The implications of this are very significant. As we have already discussed, all 2-year-olds are striving to make themselves understood in order to get their needs met and to make friends. If their journey is made more arduous through the difficulties described above then the child's behaviour may become increasingly disruptive, attracting a lot of negative attention. This then reinforces their feeling of not fitting in to this new environment impacting negatively on their sense of belonging and self-esteem.

Alternatively, the child may give up and withdraw into themselves. The silent, passive 2-year-old in a busy group of 2 to 5-year-olds can be so easily overlooked and thought of as quiet but fine. Only close Key Person relationships, careful observation and good communication with parents to gauge what home conversation is like will pick this up. Settings where different ways of communicating are embraced wholeheartedly by children and practitioners alike can provide rich inclusive environments in which all children thrive.

Knowing each individual child's language journey

All these issues point to the importance of knowing the developmental journey each 2-year-old is on. Because young children's language is immature and often individual (as in the case study of Jack below), the carer needs to know each child really well. Naturally, practitioners will never have the in-depth knowledge of the primary carer. Equally, nor will the primary carer understand every reference the child makes to the setting. However, by working closely together they will be able to learn as much as they can and thereby reduce those times of frustration when 2-year-olds cannot make those closest to them understand what it is they want to tell them.

Case study

During an outing Jack (2y6m) is on the platform as a steam train arrives. He loves Thomas the Tank Engine and so this outing was thought to be ideal as he would so enjoy going on a real steam train. But as the steam gushes out and is very noisy, Jack tries to explain why he couldn't possibly go on the train. He is drawing on his limited knowledge of scariness to explain:

J: Locodiles (crocodiles) in trees (pointing upwards).
KP: What crocodiles?
J: Locodiles (crocodiles) in trees might go on the track! (Jack is frowning, he is obviously not joking.)

The context to this baffling story is that crocodiles have been a regular theme in his play. He pretends to be a crocodile using his arms as the crocodile jaws, or a pair of kitchen tongs to 'attack' his playmate. He initiates play where the adult is the crocodile and chases after him.

This is an interesting example of a 2-year-old's language development. Jack has quite a sophisticated grasp of grammar (e.g. 'might go on') alongside the common difficulty a younger child might have with pronouncing certain phonemes like the 'k' sound beginning 'crocodile', although, by 2y6m Jack's word 'locodile' might be more his own creation and preference for what he wants to call this animal (Gillen 1999) rather than any inability, especially as he pronounces the 'k' in the middle. But imagine the resulting negative consequences had the context not been known by the adults that were with Jack. In contrast to the explanations and reassurance he received, feelings of embarrassment, annoyance and despair could have overwhelmed him. Added to which, Jack would also have had the anxiety that if he could not make himself understood, he might be snapped up, train and all, by a 'locodile'! Fortunately Jack, like most 2-year-olds, also had some very clear physical ways of making his fear understood, pulling away to the back of the platform. However, such physical means of expression can be exhausting and upsetting for the child and those caring for them. So, practitioners, who understand the context, empathize with children's fears and confusions, and those who can respect the child's wishes, are contributing much more to the well-being of the child.

Jack's family encouraged his speech from early on. However, Brice-Heath's (1983) research found cultural differences in this regard. Some believe that talk emerges naturally and does not need to be taught and they have no expectation that the very young will learn words (Brice-Heath 1983). Neither is there any great significance attached to early attempts to talk. The child is loved, cared for and enjoyed but talked about in their presence more than talked to; yet out of this, emerges a confident talker (Brice-Heath 1983).

If practitioners have little understanding of such diverse but equally beneficial ways to promote communication skills, then they may exhibit disapproval and a desire to 'educate' a family with a different approach. This does not facilitate the mutual respect that underpins good partnership and for parents can make handing their child over to these professionals even more daunting than usual.

Both the example we saw in Nina's family and the findings of Brice-Heath (1983) demonstrate how social interaction is at the heart of language. The temptation in an early years setting is to create opportunities to 'teach' language, especially if this is perceived to be lacking. For example, some settings have replaced key group or 'Island time' with language groups where the children are not necessarily with their Key Person. This could result in language being divorced from context, making communication and language development more difficult for the 2-year-old.

Creating interesting language environment and excursions

Recently there has been a great deal of concern about young children's poor communications skills on entering early years' settings. A poll carried out by

ICAN (2004) reported in National Literacy Trust (2004) found that 89 per cent of nursery workers asked said that they thought preschool children's speech and language ability had deteriorated and 94 per cent attributed this to the amount of time adults and children spend talking together. A number of initiatives to address concerns about language and communication development have been implemented. One such was Every Child a Talker (ECAT) (DCSF 2008b) which was a £40 million government programme for those who work with young children on supporting early language development. The Early Language Development Programme (ELDP), then aimed to build on what ECAT had achieved by training and supporting early years workers, particularly those working with children under 3 and in disadvantaged areas.

In spite of these initiatives, other structural pressures can be seen to undermine practitioners' good intentions on this front. For example, a student on placement at a nursery commented on how excited the children were to see her each week. She said that this was probably because she had time to chat and play with them as the practitioners were so busy with all the work they had to do! When questioned about the nature of this work, she replied that it was all the record keeping and planning they have to keep up to date so they are not in trouble with the manager and Ofsted. Yet the most effective strategy for fostering communication and language is not engaging in reams of paperwork but rather it is creating a 'warm language environment' (Abbott and Langston 2005) and one interesting enough to inspire comment, questions and discussion. This would include ensuring that there are many connections between home and the early years setting such as photos of children's pets displayed at eye level, play materials and real objects that the practitioners knows a child has at home.

Effective practice in this respect would also include the following:

- A book area with a variety of books on a rug and surrounded by cushions or with a comfortable settee where practitioners and children can sit comfortably together
- Small photo albums containing photographs from home and the setting
- A laptop or tablet computer with songs and stories recorded by children's parents/carers in their home languages and accents
- Enclosed, sound-absorbing, cosy areas perhaps with a canopy made with colourful fabric.

Frequently going on short local outings is also a very useful strategy for stimulating shared memories and conversations. Photos can be taken at each stage and then the walk relived when these are displayed. If this is at child level and on a Velcro strip children can sequence and re-sequence them, building their understanding of narrative.

Having visitors such as pets brought to the early years setting also provokes talk. Introducing them in a separate room in case children are fearful or allergic or the pet gets overwhelmed is a useful idea. Then taking a small group of children to visit at a time will enable practitioners to support those who want to touch the animal, find its different body parts and compare with their own, see its food and how it eats, know what its name is, or even discuss its poo (a subject of great interest to 2-year-olds). Subsequent stories featuring this animal could be used or the choice of pet may have reflected a current favourite story or rhyme in the first place.

Such activities are rich opportunities for children's language and communication skills to flourish. Abundant talk is also enhanced when practitioners put children's actions into words and describe their thinking, and when they wonder aloud with children rather than ask questions that require a 'right' answer, such as 'I wonder what the tortoise is eating?' rather than 'What is that the tortoise is eating?' This fosters a spirit of enquiry, reasoning and problem-solving.

Conclusion

Helping young children to become competent, confident talkers is a valuable gift. They are helped and supported in this journey by practitioners who understand paths of language development and who know the individual children they work with well. These practitioners tune into all the ways 2-year-olds (who have limited but growing vocabulary and idiosyncratic ways of talking) communicate. They provide just the right amount of what Wood et al. (1976) refer to as scaffolding to support and sustain a conversation, whilst enabling the child to build up their linguistic repertoire. However, they are also aware of the stumbling blocks for 2-year-olds in group settings and how these can be circumnavigated. In this way they are clear about the important role they play in enabling the child to become an articulate adult.

Through attentive listening, practitioners and parents support 2-year-olds in refining their language skills as a means of getting their needs met, expressing emotion, remembering and building relationships.

6   Losing our way: coping with confusion and conflict

Introduction

When confronted by repeated changes and continuously new experiences that we have little control over, in a situation that is unfamiliar and/or overwhelmingly loud and busy, or where we feel stressed but have little support, even the most mature of us 'lose it' from time to time. It is therefore not surprising that for 2-year-olds with much less experience, knowledge and understanding of the physical and social world and with far fewer social and communication skills, getting confused and feeling stressed are common and can result in emotional collapses.

As explored in Chapters 1 and 4, a main focus of a 2-year-old's learning is about what it means to be 'me'; they have come to understand that they can cause things to happen, do things on their own and get strong reactions from people, as Greenman et al. (2008: 58) say, practitioners can therefore expect 2-year-olds to 'act powerful' and 'be contrary'. In addition, they experience their feelings with great intensity, which can easily overpower their self-control and ability to keep others' needs in mind. These emotions, combined with their immature social skills and limited language, often put them on a collision course with those around them (Manning-Morton and Thorp 2003, 2006). This chapter will explore the developmental processes underpinning 2-year-olds 'losing their way' and also discuss strategies that will help practitioners not to 'lose *their* way' when responding to 2-year-olds struggling with these challenges.

Case study

Lenny (2y4m) and Marco (2y2m) have both been at their early years setting for six months; they share the same interests but often get into conflict when in proximity to each other. Practitioners are on alert for this as both children's parents complain that their child is hurt by the other.

Lenny picks up a tool box from the home corner and then puts it down while he goes to find a hard hat from the box. While Lenny is choosing the hat, Marco takes the tool box and starts playing with it. Lenny comes back and finds Marco is playing with the tool box. Lenny shouts, 'Gimme, gimme.' Marco ignores Lenny. Lenny tries to snatch the tool box. Marco confronts him and says, 'No.' Lenny grabs it and pushes him away. Marco falls backwards and starts crying. Ella, a practitioner, intervenes: 'No, Lenny, we don't push our friends. Give it back please.' Lenny ignores her. She moves him away and gives him 'time out'.

Lenny throws himself on the floor, kicking and crying. Julie, his Key Person, comes and sits next to him. She had noticed that he had been playing with the tool box and sympathizes with his feelings of frustration. She explains that Marco did not know he had only gone to fetch the Bob the Builder hat. She reminds Lenny in a friendly way that it's not very nice to push people and better to say, 'Mine please, Marco!' or get Ella or her to help. Lenny looks the other way. Julie gives him a cuddle and asks, 'Shall we go and find another tool box or see if Marco has finished?' Lenny says, 'No!' and cries louder. Julie strokes his back and says, 'I'll give you a minute to get over it' and turns back to the adjacent play activity.

A minute later, Julie hears that Lenny is calming down; she turns back and asks him, 'Do you want to come now?' Lenny nods his head and gets up from the floor. He holds Julie's hand and goes back to the home corner. Marco is playing with a hand bag and the tool box is on the floor. Julie picks up the tool box and asks Lenny, 'Can you say sorry to Marco? Then we can play with the tool box.' Lenny hesitates at first but pats Marco's shoulder. Julie accepts this attempt to say sorry saying, 'That's nice, Lenny.' Lenny looks at Julie and smiles while heading off to play with the tool box. Julie says, 'Marco, you didn't know Lenny was playing with it, did you? Well done for just saying no and not hitting.'

Agreeing a starting point

Children at 2 years old like Marco and Lenny are often labelled as 'terrible twos' and their behaviour termed 'challenging' but these stereotyped views are unhelpful in every way. 'Challenging behaviour' suggests a deliberate attempt is being made by the child to be difficult, while 'terrible twos' suggests an inevitability of a difficult year that carers just have to grit their teeth and get through. These views deny the immense social and emotional learning that is taking place in the third year of life, one which requires knowledgeable support, rather than minimizing or disregard. Many of the behaviours arising from the characteristics of 2-year-olds, such as limited social skills and language (Stonehouse 1990), can be exacerbated by being in a group of other 2-year-olds with the same characteristics, as seen in the case study above. Therefore knowledge and understanding about how young children behave and why will enable practitioners to plan appropriately; to empathize when things go wrong; to be less likely to get into a battle of wills situation and so more likely to experience job satisfaction. This is evident in Julie's efforts to adopt the kind of partnership approach (Lieberman 1995) described in the observation above. It may have been time-consuming, but her patience and self-control led to her creating a secure calm-down space rather than a time out place where children are simply excluded from play and punished for being immature negotiators at age 2! Her ability to show empathy and give choices yet maintain the boundaries of the behaviour that she expects helps Lenny to cooperate with his pride and self-respect intact and to usefully learn about his emotions and behaviours and how they impact on others. This approach also gives Julie positive feedback and so enhances her professional esteem.

However, it is unhelpful if only Julie adopts this approach while Ella adopts another, or indeed if they have not agreed an approach with Lenny's and Marco's parents, as this will lead to inconsistency and confusion for the children. Practitioners working in a team need to develop a shared pedagogical approach which is not restricted to writing a policy, which alone will not ensure consistent appropriate practice in responding to a 2-year-old's behaviour. Practice is more effective if viewed as an ongoing approach and one that includes team members and parents sharing their views on what discipline, boundaries or managing behaviour means to them. Words or terms in relation to behaviour have different connotations for different people but often are thought to be just about rule keeping or rewards and punishment. Gerber (2005: 42) uses a much more helpful definition, seeing discipline as: 'a social contract, in which family or community members agree to accept and obey a particular set of rules'. What is important is that this 'social contract' really reflects the needs of the particular members of the community, which in this case is 2-year-olds. For example, practitioners who are not aware of 2-year-olds' needs and characteristics, or settings new to taking 2-year-olds may develop a set of rules that set them up to fail, such as: all sitting nicely, not playing with cutlery while waiting for their meal to arrive, which is bound to trip up the busy, curious and active 2-year-old. With this in mind, the next section considers the kinds of behaviours that arise from 2-year-olds' key characteristics and suggests responses and strategies that reflect a partnership approach.

Understanding the characteristics of 2-year-olds and their behaviours

With their fondness for mobility, 2-year-olds are often on the move, enjoying pulling, pushing, running and climbing. They are enjoying the newfound freedom of being able to go off independently and thereby trying out being separate from others (Manning-Morton and Thorp 2003). Hence when an adult calls them, they may take off in the opposite direction, glancing back to see the adult's reaction. This of course, is fine if the physical boundaries are in place to prevent the child coming to harm, such as a park or open green space but not so fine if on a busy road!

Equally, as Piaget (1952a) and Gopnik et al. (1999) have both described, 2-year-olds are like researchers or little scientists: always investigating and wanting hands-on experience and proof of what they are told and what they see. This often involves taking things apart, which of course is an important part of the process of finding out how things work, but doesn't always include putting things back together again! This characteristic includes exploring their identity as a separate person, so, when a child is asked not to touch something, they may look at the adult and do it one more time anyway, for example. Again, this is fine when there are safe but interesting items in reach to explore but more risky when there are harmful substances, items or environments.

The first response of practitioners to these behaviours, as with all behaviours, is to make sure that the physical and psychological environments are adapted to cater for these characteristics. For example, knowledge that the 2-year-old is exploring being a separate person and being independent and not trying to be difficult helps practitioners not to over-react. Mckay (cited in Stonehouse 1988) advises reacting to many situations with humour as it can distract and diffuse a situation without setting up a conflict. Often it is sufficient to just restate the boundaries calmly with a simple explanation, then offer an alternative and move with the child to another space or remove the hazardous item (Manning-Morton and Thorp 2003, 2006).

Having clear, reasonable boundaries that are implemented and reinforced consistently helps 2-year-olds feel safe and contained. They may react with confusion and erratic behaviour if there are inconsistencies or sudden changes. For example, after learning more about 2-year-olds, Nikki thought that her team's approach to managing their regular outing to the park playground was too restrictive. She wanted to support the children's autonomy and independence, so decided to let them walk across the park without holding hands. The children then ran off in all directions, some towards the gate and the street beyond! Upon reflection, Nikki realized that she should have talked to the children about this change beforehand and been clear about her expectations. She also saw that she needed to agree with her colleagues how they would work together to balance the children's freedom to roam with the need to keep them safe.

As discussed in Chapter 4, 2-year-olds are in the very early stages of learning how to balance others' needs with their own and how to assert themselves in socially acceptable ways. This means that they often assert themselves badly, for example, taking a toy from another child and hitting out if resisted, just like Lenny and Marco. Responding with empathy, advice and fairness, as Julie did in the case study, can help the child to find acceptable ways to assert themselves.

A 2-year-old is feeling the edges of their autonomy in this way; this means that they sometimes also assert their independence when it's not necessarily in their interests. They may struggle with making choices and frequently change their minds, for example, saying 'No' to something they really want or asking for custard on their pudding, then wailing with dismay when it is poured on, saying they don't want it. These can be baffling and frustrating characteristics for the practitioner but are part of the exploration and experimentation involved in learning to be an autonomous decision-maker. This can be hard even for adults who are comparably mature decision-makers, yet who struggle over dessert menus, for example (Manning-Morton and Thorp 2003). For children, this process is best supported by practitioners who build opportunities for choice and decision-making into the day and who make sure that choices are manageable, such as giving a child two or three choices rather than a huge range of alternatives. In addition, a 2-year-old, when asked if they would like some fruit, may not understand that the social rule is that you only take one piece! It is a lack of understanding of these social rules that often trip them up. A 2-year-old entering a setting will have made tremendous gains in understanding, however, there is still much to confuse. For example, participating in finger painting is encouraged but smearing food over the table results in a practitioner's disapproval. Experimenting with squirting bottles in the water play is celebrated but spraying the toilet with wee is heavily discouraged. Obviously practitioners must teach children what things are fine to do and where, but need to do this with understanding of the confusion in the child's mind and with explanations rather than condemnation.

In this way, 2-year-olds gradually learn how to be part of a social group. Practitioners often concentrate on the ability to share and take turns as the focus of social learning, yet these skills are a very small part of developing social understanding. Moreover, a 2-year-olds' development of 'mindsight' (Siegel 1999: 149) and understanding of time means that being able to understand and accept these concepts varies hugely. Practitioners sometimes say, 'You must share,' or 'If you can't share, you can't have it at all!' But the same practitioner would not be punitive towards a 2-year-old who was not yet able to add up or do cartwheels. Also, it is probable that the practitioner also has possessions that they wouldn't dream of sharing! Understanding 2-year-olds' social development helps practitioners not to have unrealistic expectations of them in this respect. Instead effective practice includes developing strategies such as offering exciting alternatives, having more than one popular item and most important, being trustworthy. This means explaining turn taking, ensuring there is only a short interval to wait and always keeping your word. So when a practitioner promises that a 2-year-old 'can have a turn next' or 'can do more painting after lunch', that is what must happen, or next time why should they comply? When 2-year-olds can rely on their close adults to manage such negotiations and compromises in a fair and just way, they learn that delayed gratification does not mean no gratification and thereby gradually learn that waiting and turn taking can aid their friendships.

A central issue in the behaviours of 2-year-olds is their impulsiveness and apparent lack of self-control. These behaviours can be understood in the context of the very gradual maturation of the area of the brain that processes the conscious control of emotions. Understanding that self-control develops gradually and can fluctuate enables practitioners to have appropriate expectations, one of which is to expect, for example, that although Marco showed self-control and resisted the temptation to hit out at Lenny this morning, this does not mean he could always do so. Later that day, for example, he was unable to resist taking raisins from another child's plate. So 2-year-olds often show that they know what not to do, but can't always not do it. Adults who have tried dieting or stopping smoking will understand this well. In this way practitioners can also come to understand that emotions and behaviours in 2-year-olds are also very physical experiences; they feel their emotions and express them through physical actions, as explained below.

Emotional regulation and the brain

Emotions are governed by the limbic system at the centre of the brain, which is densely connected to the inner core of the cortex (the outermost sheet of neural tissue where most of the information processing in the brain takes place), where emotions are consciously felt and understood.

The amygdale (a set of neurons located deep in limbic system of the brain) is described by LeDoux (1998) and Goleman (1996) as being the part of the brain that is our 'emotional sentinel' (Goleman 1996: 17); its function is protective, to aid escape from danger. When the brain receives information that is threatening to our survival in some way, rather than being transmitted to the cortex for consideration, it travels directly to the amygdale where basic emotions such as fear and anger trigger the fight or flight response. Daniel Goleman (1996) describes in detail how anger causes a rush of adrenaline which generates energy for vigorous action, as does fear, which also triggers a flood of hormones that put our bodies on alert. When we feel happy, there is increased activity in brain circuits that inhibit negative feelings and increase energy, while sadness makes us slow down and want to retreat to a safe place. In this way we can see how emotions are a bodily phenomenon, as areas of the brain concerned with feelings coincide with structures that represent and regulate body states (Carroll 2001).

As more and more connections are made between neurons as a result of the child's experience of the world and relationships with other people, pre-existing feelings start to become conscious at around 6 months old (Carter 1998). It takes about two years before the dendrites of the neurons in the frontal lobes of the cerebral cortex are fully extended and for synapses to reach their maximum density. From then on it is a process of synaptic pruning and firming up of neural pathways as the child's emotional learning grows. This maturation of the orbitofrontal part of the pre-frontal cortex plays a key role in detecting social and emotional clues and has the capacity for developing emotional control (Gerhardt 2004) as they govern non-emergency emotional reactions by sending chemical inhibitors to the amygdale. It is negative feedback from the frontal cortex lobes that enables us to delay gratification of our needs and to exercise the kind of self-control that is necessary for successful social interactions (Carter 1998; LeDoux 1998; Eliot 1999).

However, it should be noted that this is a long, slow process. The process of myelination, which protects the neural pathways once formed, only starts at about 18 months and is not completed until late adolescence (Eliot 1999). Understanding these developmental processes helps to explain the high level of emotionality of young children and their inability to control aspects of their behaviour and expressions of emotion, as emotional regulation only gradually increases throughout childhood and adolescence into early adulthood.

In addition, because the amygdale receives and stores the potent emotional but unconscious memories of the first few years of life, these memories can be triggered by bodily and sensory experiences, and the strength of emotional memory can also cause the fight or flight response. Daniel Goleman (1996: 13) calls this 'emotional hi-jacking', where emotion overwhelms thinking. Circuits from the limbic system create neural static at times of strong emotion, which interfere with messages in the cortex, resulting in the experience of not being able to think straight or concentrate well on anything.

Challenges for practitioners

The issues raised in the theory box above mean that practitioners encountering the strong emotional outbursts of 2-year-olds need to consider carefully their understanding of the triggers for the behaviours and their responses to them. A behaviourist approach of naughty steps/ thinking time/ time-out chairs or sticker charts does not help children to sufficiently understand their feelings and behaviours. Neither does such an approach consider the kind of distressing early experiences that may be triggering a child's behaviour, which are not forgotten but stored in their bodies and unconscious minds and thus impact on their learning. It is close empathetic relationships such as between Lenny and Julie that support effective emotional learning and enable self-restraint and social understanding.

If those working with this age group consider all the complex and perplexing learning situations that 2-year-olds encounter, they will understand, have empathy with and even expect the tantrums or emotional collapses young children sometimes have. It is inevitable that sometimes a 2-year-old's fragile ego will shatter in the face of all these frustrations and misunderstandings.

Sometimes it is hard to discern whether a tantrum is an emotional collapse due to cumulative frustrations or a ploy for getting their wants supplied. Tantrums can be a very effective means to get what a child wants or to bring help and as such can be seen as a learned skill, even though it is distressing for the child, the carer and others in the group. Practitioners may be tempted to be very critical of a child using this strategy, seeing the behaviour as manipulative; but as Mckay warns, 'caregivers tend to over-use the excuse that a tantrum is a bid for attention . . . Most young children are frightened when their emotions get out of hand and usually need comfort and reassurance' (in Stonehouse 1990: 88: 72). A more positive response is to give the child an alternative way and to ensure that this is more rewarding than the tantrum. For example, in the case study Julie showed that she understood what Lenny wanted and suggested how he should go about getting it. By adopting Julie's alternative, pro-social behaviour, Lenny achieved a successful outcome: regaining the tool box.

In general, if it is not possible to agree with what a child wants, (for example, wanting to wearing slippers in the rain), it is useful to explain that there is no choice but to give the child some power in the situation within the boundaries. For example, saying 'You can wear boots or these nice red shoes' and withdrawing while they make the choice can help restore some of the child's dignity and composure. However, if the 2-year-olds in a group often have emotional collapses, as well as addressing individual children's needs, the first thing for a team to do is to re-evaluate the routines of the day, the physical environment and the quality of Key Person relationships (Manning-Morton and Thorp 2003).

Developing a partnership approach

A partnership approach relates to the concept of a social contract as mentioned earlier (Gerber 2005). It requires the needs and resources of all parties to be considered, the 2-year-old, other children in the group, the practitioners and the parents. With regard to the children, it requires seeing the setting of boundaries for children's behaviour as part of their whole social development. As Greenman and Stonehouse say, 'Discipline, guiding children's behaviour, or setting limits are all concerned with helping children learn how to take care of themselves, other people and the world around them' (1996: 138).

Practitioners new to working with younger children may consider working with 2-year-olds as the most difficult age, as their changeability and sometimes unpredictability can make practitioners fearful of losing control and therefore become more controlling. Yet if we want children to develop inner control and become adults who understand why a behaviour is anti-social or an action wrong, then we need to implement ways of guiding children's behaviour that maintain safe boundaries yet keep in mind that resisting coercion and saying 'no' is sometimes a necessary life skill. Otherwise we risk raising individuals who over-rely on others to tell them what to do.

So, rather than viewing children as needing to be trained to fit in with a set of (often unwritten) rules, it can be useful to see them as people with whom we are becoming social partners (Trevarthen 1998). Two-year-olds are practising with 'goal-corrected partnership' (Bowlby 1982, cited in Lieberman 1995), where they are beginning to understand how others' plans differ from their own. In situations where there are competing needs, the practitioner's task is to find a way of moving away from a confrontation to a negotiated agreement. By engaging in negotiation and compromise, practitioners are modelling flexibility and mutual consideration, which are vital life skills. In this way they show benevolent authority rather than control because they are interested in working alongside children, not in having power over them (Manning-Morton and Thorp 2003, 2006).

A partnership approach also includes distinguishing between serious violations and minor transgressions and mistakes. Children who are heavily berated for both small and large indiscretions will be unable to tell the difference between these. They may then be less well equipped to cope with social limitations and restriction as they go on in life and be resentful, fearful or defiant and uncooperative when expected to conform. This requires that practitioners regularly discuss the rules they apply in their setting and evaluate their validity and effectiveness. Many rules exist in settings 'because that is the way we have always done it'. So practitioners need to spend time talking to each other and to parents to ensure consistency. This kind of consistency is very different to the kind where an adult will not back down from a decision, even though it was mistaken or unnecessary. Willingness to change our minds in the face of other evidence teaches children about the value of engaging in dialogue and negotiation and about differing points of view (Lieberman 1995).

Although it has important positive outcomes for children's social learning, developing a partnership approach is not necessarily the easy option for practitioners in the short term, as it requires team work, discussion about practices that may be causing difficult behaviour in children and reflection on personal responses. Some behaviours that children exhibit trigger strong responses in their caring adults because they are reminders of what they were or were not allowed to do as children or they prompt memories of how they were treated, which might be uncomfortable. In a Key Times training exercise, practitioners are asked to identify the behaviours in children they find particularly difficult and how they make them feel. They are then asked to identify how they might or could respond if they acted *unprofessionally*. They consistently identify that the unprofessional way they could respond often mirrors the original difficult behaviour. They then consider that the feelings provoked in them are therefore likely to be the very same feelings that the child experienced that led to the behaviour that the practitioner found so difficult.

Reflective exercise

Consider the case study scenario or a similar situation you have been involved in. Identify what feelings Lenny and Marco may have been experiencing, then consider what feelings Ella and Julie may have had about Lenny's and Marco's behaviour.

- How did Ella's and Julie's behaviours reflect or substitute Lenny's and Marco's?
- Which behaviours in young children particularly bother you?
- Make some notes about why this is and how it relates to your own early experiences.
- Now consider the idea that 'all behaviour has meaning' and reflect on the possible psychological meanings of the behaviours of children you care for.

Just as Julie advised Lenny in the case study, sometimes the best thing the practitioner can do, when children's behaviours affect them deeply, is to step back and seek help. When the culture of the early years setting is one that allows practitioners to discuss their feelings and reflect on their practice, new ways of understanding the child's behaviour and a greater empathy for the child may emerge. This can result in what Taggart (2014) describes as 'Compassionate Pedagogy'. Research carried out amongst practitioners studying a level 4 certificate in Professional Practice with Children aged Birth to Three also identified that having regular individual times to discuss their work (including their own limitations and vulnerabilities) with a knowledgeable and caring manager is a key element of professional support (Thorp 2013), as this strengthened their feeling of competency and being a professional rather than making them feel professional failures.

The trouble with praise

A partnership approach also means emphasizing what children can do, not just what they cannot do and appreciating their efforts at pro-social behaviour, their acts of kindness and care towards others and the environment. Practitioners often identify praise as a key way in which they foster a positive self-concept in children; however, there are many drawbacks to praising children. Using empty, indiscriminate praise such as 'well done' or 'good girl' tells a child nothing about what they have done that is so wonderful and so doesn't help the child to understand and therefore repeat their positive behavior in other situations. In this way, praise can lead children to rely only on an authority figure's evaluation of right and wrong, rather than develop self-direction and self-control. We have long understood the importance of explaining why negative behaviours are unacceptable and of avoiding labelling, such as 'naughty boy'; the same understanding needs to be applied to praise. Indiscriminate praise can also communicate insincerity if it becomes an automatic response to almost anything the child does or says and therefore becomes meaningless. For example, a team of practitioners were observed to have adopted the habit of praising what children were doing by continuously saying 'good ... sitting/eating/listening' to the children. This kind of praise does not support children's positive self-concept or social understanding.

Praise also infers judgement and evaluation and therefore, superiority. So praise of children's achievements, although intended positively, can of course also be withdrawn or used negatively. So if practitioners praise completed paintings or reaching the top of the climbing frame with 'well done' or 'aren't you clever', what does it mean for the child to whom they haven't said this, or the same child the next time the practitioner doesn't notice? Such praise is shown to invite comparison and competition and can lead to children working in order to achieve adult praise rather than from any inner interest or motivation. At a time when self-knowledge is forming, it can lead to conformity: a child producing what the practitioner deems is valuable rather than developing their own assessment and view of their efforts (Dowling 2010).

This does not mean that children's positive behaviours are ignored but are noticed and acknowledged in more thoughtful and direct ways. For example, the High-scope Curriculum (2014) suggests that participating in children's play, encouraging children to describe their efforts and products – for example, 'Ooh, tell me about your painting' – and making specific comments such as 'Wow, you've climbed all the way to the top, that's the first time I've seen you do that!' are more effective strategies. This approach avoids using praise only for achievements of an end product such as finishing a jigsaw. It ensures instead that children are given strong messages that their efforts, perseverance and concentration are valued: messages that contribute positively to children's dispositions to learning (Katz 1993). Such dispositions are more likely to be apparent in children who have a mastery orientation (Dweck 2000), seeing things as achievable if they keep trying and practising because their motivation comes from inside them rather than from the external approval of an adult.

Working closely with parents

Developing a partnership approach to behaviour with parents is crucial as it is an area where different views are strongly held. Each family will already have their own 'social contract' (Gerber 2005: 41) and so when a new child enters a setting, encountering a set of rules and adult responses that conflict with what they have learned at home will cause confusion and children 'losing their way'. These differences can raise dilemmas for practitioners, who need to balance the need for continuity and respect for family traditions with their knowledge of child development and good practice. Equally, parents need to respect a practitioner's experience and knowledge yet ensure that their individual child's needs are responded to appropriately. All parents will be concerned for their child who either displays or experiences negative behaviours such as biting or hitting and will feel defensive and protective of their child. Where such situations occur, practitioners need to be honest but tactful. Blaming each other or individual children is not helpful in this situation but a review of provision and a clear strategy to support all the children involved is necessary. Parents may feel embarrassed and powerless when faced by a professional reporting on their child's behaviour. So practitioners should always think carefully about when and where they talk to a parent as well as their approach. Adopting an attitude of: 'This is a tricky situation for both of us, let's plan a way forward together' will be much more disarming than a more confrontational approach and more productive as it will value the family's input.

Conclusion

Many of the everyday behaviours that have given 2-year-olds a negative reputation arise from the common characteristics of their development and learning that they share. Developing greater knowledge and understanding of these allows practitioners to be more able to respond appropriately, to be less likely to attribute blame to the child, parents or colleagues, and to plan their provision more effectively. Adopting a partnership approach and a more thoughtful approach to praise will better support young children's social understanding and their group belonging. Practitioners who have support from colleagues and managers through being given time to reflect and discuss their concerns, struggles and successes with their professional challenges are more likely to experience job satisfaction and positive professional esteem. The sympathetic pedagogy that can result from this can empower children and practitioners.

7 Active exploration on the move

Introduction

The idea of movement is absolutely central to thinking about a 2-year-old's journey in life and in an early years setting. For most 2-year-olds, running, climbing, rolling and jumping are not just what they want to do but what they need to do. This chapter will explore this enthusiasm for being 'on the go' and other significant aspects of the 2-year-old's physicality, such as the remarkable level of physical change taking place in the 2-year-old's brain.

A challenge that this aspect of 2-year-olds' development presents to practitioners and parents is how to keep these adventurers safe whilst enabling them to be independent and take risks. Being so physically active is tiring as well as exciting, so practitioners need to understand the challenges that face 2-year-olds on this part of the journey and provide the close physical contact upon which 2-year-olds thrive too. All these factors of course are intrinsically linked, an appreciation of which will go a long way to informing effective provision. Hopefully, informed provision arises from discussion and policies based on theory, keen observation and regular evaluation. So this chapter will also consider how such underpinning perspectives impact on the quality of 2-year-olds' journeys.

> **Case study**
>
> Shannon (2y2m) is cautious about physical play and looks to her Key Person Kirsty for reassurance. Shannon has Downs Syndrome and whilst she has been walking for six months, she often trips and falls over and collides with things. She attends the setting three days a week. Her mother and grandma are very worried about her getting hurt in a busy group setting. They prefer her

to use the buggy on outings and stay away from the climbing apparatus in the garden. Kirsty is spending time with them explaining what Shannon learns from being outdoors and sharing photos and videos of her play outside.

* * *

Angelina and Alexio are non-identical twins (2y10m) at the same setting as Shannon and they are Polish. Angelina is very confident and likes to leap on her Key Person and on her friends for affectionate hugs. However, this brings her into conflict with them on occasions. Angelina tends to seek out new physical challenges with great enthusiasm. Her latest is trying to walk up and down the slide. Alexio also explores the nursery freely, though he is less keen on rough and tumble play or hugging. He enjoys climbing into things and watching what is happening around him before joining in.

Perspectives on physical development

In the UK and many western countries, understanding of how children's physical development takes place stems from Gesell's Maturation Theory (Crain 1992). Practitioners who are strong adherents of this perspective, which sees all developmental processes as coming from within the child, might be over-concerned with charting children's progress in relation to set milestones and with planning narrowly focussed activities that practise particular skills such as setting out cones for Shannon to practise pushing a buggy between, rather than the physically challenging and interesting outing that Kirsty took Shannon on, as described later in this chapter. Alternatively, practitioners with this perspective may see their role as largely one of just providing physical care and resources, believing development to naturally unfold. They may also be less aware of the interconnectedness of all areas of development and consider the influence of children's social and cultural experiences as less significant than their genetic make-up. So Shannon's lack of confidence might be attributed solely to the Down's Syndrome rather than the messages she receives from her mother and grandmother. On the other hand practitioners who embrace an interactionist perspective on development will view the child as a powerful actor in their own development (Miller and Pound 2011) and consider the influence of the socio-cultural environment. They will therefore recognize the contribution they make to each child's journey, so will, for example, provide for Alexio's interest in being enclosed and take his more considered response to physical games into account in their expectations.

Maturational and dynamic systems perspectives

Gesell (1880–1961) suggested that biological forces underpin the momentum for a child's physical development providing a 'genetically determined, naturally unfolding course of growth' (cited in Berk 2009: 12). He established norms of development by observing children and identifying general patterns, which he saw as universal and invariant. The ages and stages identified by Gesell inform books that focus on developmental milestones such as the one by Sheridan et al. (2007) and early years curricular guidance such as the Early Years Foundation Stage Guidance (EYFS) (DFE 2014a) which has supporting 'Development Matters' tables (BAECE 2012) to help practitioners know what to expect of children at different ages.

The dynamic systems perspective (Thelen and Smith 1994) sees physical change happening as a result of a complex system of forces operating together, including cognition, perception, motivation and children's social worlds as well as biological imperatives. It recognizes children's ability to adapt their behaviour in response to these forces to gain maximum effect (Berk 2009). Thelen (1995, cited in Schaffer 2006) argues that any new movement or motor skill is a 'final common pathway', a result of these systems operating together.

Brain development

By the age of 2 there has already been considerable activity in the brain. The brain grows more rapidly than any other body part in the first 12 months of life, tripling its volume and becoming three-quarters of its full adult size (Karmiloff-Smith 1994). Every brain cell or neuron is present at birth, but unlike other species the synapses that make neural connections are not yet established (Karmiloff-Smith 1994). The second and third years are also times of rapid synapto-genesis (growth of connections). However, by the third year synaptic pruning is also taking place; children lose the connections that they do not use and more room is available for well-used connections to be firmed up through a process of myelination which consolidates neural pathways. Synapses, synaptic genesis, synaptic pruning and myelination are all terms describing neurological processes which regulate and facilitate changes in the brain. Hundreds of dendrites branch out from each neuron ready to receive messages from axons sent out from another neuron. Synapses are the microscopic gaps that allow electrical impulses to pass between the connecting dendrite and axon (Carter 1998). Myelination is the process of a protective sheath forming around the connecting nerve fibres which makes the passage of messages between neurons more effective (Carter 1998).

The sensations and stimulation of movement in physical activity all play a significant part in enabling the connections between the billions of neurons present in the brain to be made. We cannot separate the brain from the complex network of the body. The brain, like a tree, has roots which are distributed throughout the body, through the spinal cord, the autonomic nervous system and the neuroendocrine system, which are vital in carrying messages to and from the brain. In this way, the brain is a complex network of feedback loops that gives our bodies vital instructions. But the brain also depends on the three-dimensional dynamic structure of the body. Not only does the body orient us in time and space (proprioception), it also provides a feedback loop of representations to the brain. For example, muscle is packed with proprioceptors measuring changes in muscle tension, pressure and the position of limbs in space. These create a constantly updated dynamic map of the body in the mind. So proprioception strengthens the sense of 'this is me' and the body becomes central to the ability to think (Carroll 2004).

A 'systems' perspective on development sees the mind and body as interdependent. This is different to a standard linear (and hierarchical) model in which development goes from managing basic regulatory functions, through emotional landmarks to increasing cognitive and verbal skills (Schaffer 2006). However, although not linear or applicable to all children, there is a general overarching pattern of physical development in the early years of life, which sees neuro-muscular control gradually progressing from the head downwards (cephalo-caudal development) and from the trunk outwards to fingertips and toes (proximo-distal development). By 2, children's agility and dexterity will have usually developed extensively as a result of the leg kicking, arm waving, rolling, sitting, crawling, walking and grasping that have been practised continuously for the previous two years (Bee 2000; Smith et al. 2011) but it remains that these early physical skills are still to be refined. For example, the refinement of dexterity in the hands is still maturing at age 5, which has implications for expectations regarding pencil control.

Physical development: the engine that powers all aspects of the journey

The physical maturation of 2-year-olds can be seen in the way they seem to lose their baby chubbiness; this is because fat is being converted to muscle. Also, their legs lengthen and they become more upright. Their previous toddling walk is replaced by heel to toe walking and the ability to run and jump emerges as arches in the feet develop and their knees and ankles gain greater flexibility (Karmiloff-Smith 1994). In relation to their dexterity, their hand and eye coordination is progressing and the crucial pincer grasp has long been added to the 2-year-old's repertoire of manual skills. Most important is the ability to use these different skills in coordination with each other, such as being able to climb or steer prams.

But of course it is not just the maturation of the nervous system and muscle fibres that enables 2-year-olds to reach this level of physical skill, it is also their insatiable appetite to explore and control their own body and it is the physical play experiences, environment and opportunities that support and motivate their physical learning.

In addition, such physical learning and development are, of course, closely interlinked with all other aspects of development and learning. This is obvious in the link between the 2-year-old's physical development and cognition, as physical encounters with new exciting experiences stimulate the neural connections in their brains and the conceptual connections in their minds as discussed earlier. Also clear is the support that growing dexterity gives to their creativity and ability to represent as they become skilled in the use of a range of tools for music and mark making, and so on. Perhaps less tangible, although still highly influential, is the link between the 2-year-old's physical and social development. Rapidly increasing agility and dexterity provide increased opportunities for social interaction, as it enables them to approach, imitate, follow and retreat from other children. They have more control over how physically close they are to their Key Person, including being able to escape from their close supervision! As they discover the physical control they now have and enjoy what their bodies can do, their sense of self and confidence grows. This can be stifled or enhanced by the disapproval or encouragement of others, when they attempt, for example, to pour a drink at snack or go head first down the slide.

The idea of physical activity as fostering all-round development is a relatively new concept. Historically physical play was regarded as just something to allow young children to 'let off steam' so that then they could then sit down and concentrate on real learning activities (Spencer, cited in Manning-Morton and Thorp 2003). Parents and practitioners may still encounter early years setting settings where this belief holds sway, even though it is not part of written policy, nor found in government guidance such as the EYFS (DFE 2014a) in the UK or the *Pre-Birth to Three: Positive Outcomes for Scotland's Children and Families* (Education Scotland 2010). But the tell-tale signs can be detected in everyday practices. For example, outdoor play may be offered for only a few short periods and planning and resourcing of the outdoor provision given far less attention. Practitioners' comments such as, 'Come and finish your work and then you can go out and play' also reveal that less value is placed on running, climbing and free movement than activities for which the child must be seated.

Practices and provision that support physical well-being

A setting that really values physical play will not only provide rich opportunities for this to happen outdoors but will also ensure that slides, climbing frames, tunnels, dens and large empty boxes and crates will be available indoors too. In the UK and some other countries, adverse weather may deter practitioners from offering as much outdoor play as compared to Australia, for example. However, providing suitable clothing will enable the 2-year-old to enjoy the sensory experiences of rain drops, puddles, wind and snow. Many settings in the UK are now adopting a 'Forest school' approach. Samuel (2012) describes how they: 'seek to encourage, motivate, engage and inspire children through positive outdoor experiences. Forest schools are closely entwined with the concepts of free flow play and learning from play.' In a Forest School approach, children learn through being encouraged to be independent, free to follow their own interests, and to engage in play that includes risk taking. A wealth of different activities can take place outside that promote sustained concentration and deep involvement, thereby supporting all-round development (Samuel 2012).

Other practitioners are introducing 'Developmental Movement Play' into their settings (Greenland 2009). Practitioners and students of early childhood will be familiar with fostering the development of the five main senses. However, there are also the vestibular and proprioceptive senses to be mindful of. As LeVoguer and Pasch (2014: 100) point out: 'the vestibular sense is a balance mechanism ... dedicated to posture, equilibrium, muscle tone and spatial orientation'. Goddard-Blythe (2004) asserts that providing rich opportunities for movement alongside good nutrition supports children's learning and aids them in becoming well balanced in all aspects of development. As Greenland (2005) found, without a strong movement vocabulary children may have limited expressive ability, inappropriate reactions to the environment and an inability to integrate cognitive skills with motor and sensory skills; this adversely affects how fluidly they can think.

Developmental Movement Play emphasizes two important aspects of movement: opportunities for children to revel in child-led, free-flow spontaneous movement play, and attention to specific early movement patterns and activities that appear to prompt neurological development. This play is concerned with facilitating the following ways of moving: floor play on backs and tummies; belly crawling; crawling; pulling, pushing, stretching, hand buffeting; and spinning, tipping and tilting (Greenland 2009). Each of these is identified as having neurological and other developmental benefits. For example, belly crawling is beneficial for stimulating horizontal eye tracking and the nerves that pull the eyes into alignment (Greenland 2009). It also strengthens the arches in the feet and promotes stability of the neck, spine and hips and gives rise to a feeling of 'vertical through-ness which helps the child to feel grounded' (Pasch 2013: 3). Crawling promotes eye–hand coordination, helps shoulder, hip and wrist rotation and supports the development of connections between the brain's two hemispheres, whose functions include memory retrieval, sorting and sequencing (Pasch 2013).

Therefore, floor play on backs and on tummies seems to be of fundamental importance and advantageous if embedded in continuous provision. Pedagogically, movement play incorporates theories of sensory integration with dance theories (Sherborne 1990) and free-flow play (Bruce 2001). It sees movement as our first language and as a direct way of communicating throughout the lifespan (Fraleigh 1999; LaBarre 2001; Bloom 2006), all of which add weight to the argument for active exploration and against expecting young children to sit at activities in order for valuable learning to take place.

Reflective exercise

Make a list of ideas for implementing movement play.

- What resources would be useful?
- What would be your main considerations/concerns?

You may have included some of the following practical ideas, which reflect those recommended by the Jabadao Developmental Movement Play Report (Greenland 2009):

- Create floor space where children can move freely.
- Have lots of cushions of varying sizes and exercise balls for whole-body rolling, sitting and bouncing.
- Develop a collection of ribbons, silk and chiffon scarves to dance twirl and wave with.
- Make tunnels from large colourful or see-through material anchored to the floor and model belly crawling through them.
- Use cardboard boxes with strings attached and empty water bottles, and other materials for children to fill and drag along.
- Set out rows of tables for children to crawl under with incentives along the way, and initiate a crawl around the room, or around the nursery garden.

- Set up bars to swing from like monkey bars indoors from door frames as well as outside.
- Provide seesaws, soft foam for indoors, and round-bottomed containers to rock and tilt in.
- Play games to music: being tall giraffes, octopuses with tentacles, curled up hedgehogs, jumping starfish.
- Encourage crouching/squatting (at all ages) by putting activities and resources on the floor.
- Make the most of grassy areas and slopes outdoors for rolling and tumbling.

Rough and tumble play

A kind of movement play that children and parents have always engaged in is 'rough and tumble' play. It is evident in the play of young animals and humans and Jarvis (2009: 177) describes it as 'cross-cultural' and 'cross-generational' play. Many 2-year-olds enjoy tightly hugging, pushing, pulling and rolling with other children. They also enjoy being thrown up in the air and being caught and tickled by their trusted adults and Bowlby (2005) suggests that such play contributes towards the close bond between carers and children.

In this way, 'rough and tumble' play is well recognized as a source of great enjoyment and an important part of young children's growing awareness of their bodies, what they can do and what happens when they come into contact with others (Goldschmeid and Selleck 1996; Panksepp 1998; Lamont 2009; Pasch 2013). The Jabadao (2011) website sums this up well and also introduces the difficulties in providing it:

> Far from breeding aggression and chaos, rough and tumble play is an important part of a joyful learning environment. It contributes to young children's physical, emotional and social development. For the adults in charge, however, it can be a real challenge.

One of the challenges for practitioners is that rough and tumble play can seem like evidence of aggressive or wild behaviour likely to escalate and 'end in tears', as many parents warn. In fact this is true to some extent as 2-year-olds are still experimenting with their own strength, and how to exercise control. They are still discovering how others may feel differently, for example, about being hugged than they do, and they are in the very early stages of understanding social boundaries. Yet allowing this kind of play will facilitate all this important learning. Pasch (2013) describes how this play helps young children learn to discern social cues, regulate their impulses and develop empathy. However, practitioners' and parents' fears cannot be overlooked, so these need to be discussed by the staff team and policies agreed that reflect both children's and practitioners' need for safety *and* children's need for physical contact.

Case study

Kirsty described how Angelina particularly enjoys launching herself off the climbing frame for her to catch. Kirsty confessed that she has had to teach her to call 'Ready Kirsty?' before jumping. She added that Angelina initiates play with another child that she seems fond of by hugging him tightly until they fall on the floor together. Most of the time the child thinks this is funny, but sometimes it ends in tears so she has to remind Angelina to notice if her friend is looking or sounding upset and she has encouraged him to say 'Stop!'

One way to support safe rough and tumble play is to know how to distinguish between playful and mutually enjoyable behaviour and aggressive and oppressive behaviour. The children participating in the former will have smiling faces (Pasch 2013) and laugh and shriek with excitement, not pain. There will be a degree of mutual pulling, pushing and rolling on each other, not dominated by one child with the other as the victim. After the play the children are likely to continue to play together. This is a sign of them bonding rather than falling out. Gently separating them at times and pointing out facial expressions or the complaints of one of the participants to the other will help this understanding to grow. Adults engaging in rough and tumble play will also help children to learn control whilst enjoying the play as long as the practitioner is attuned to when the child's excitement tips over into anxiety and they allow the child to call a halt to the game when they wish.

The more opportunities all young children have to move, the more they will become 'physically literate' (Maude 2001: 6). This includes developing the sophisticated muscle control that it takes to be able to still their bodies. A daily routine that requires 2-year-olds to sit still for prolonged periods undermines their efforts to master control of their bodies (Manning-Morton and Thorp 2003). Those practitioners new to accepting 2-year-olds into their settings may struggle to accommodate these younger children in the kind of circle times and whole group story times they have previously implemented as they may find it hard to get the 2-year-old to sit still and listen. Some practitioners might believe that this can be learnt through more sitting still. However, Maude (2001), Davies (2003) and those who have taken on board the underpinning values of movement play would argue the exact opposite and would see being able to be still as the peak of physical development only achieved through movement (Goddard-Blythe 2004).

What about the risks?

The main challenge that practitioners face when implementing movement play is their own, their colleagues' and parents' fears about the risk of children getting hurt. But while movement play and rough and tumble play seem risky activities, there is a wider concern: that is, that being risk-averse can be as, if not more, detrimental to children's all-round development. Of course practitioners must be vigilant but they should also be measured in how they respond to risky activity, as young children learn long-term lessons from the responses of their carers, such as that tackling a challenge is undesirable. The aim of movement play is to help children succeed safely in the challenges that they set themselves so that they learn better about what is and is not safe and the capabilities of their bodies and thereby take pride in their achievements. The benefits of risk are clearly identified in the Pre-Birth to Three National Guidance (Education Scotland 2010: 75) which says:

> Risk taking can be considered as 'pathways to learning' as children learn effectively from discovering what works well and what does not. Being encouraged and well supported through such experiences also helps children to understand that not getting it right first time is just a way of learning. This healthy view of play as 'trial and error' promotes resilience, improves self-esteem and helps to generate a positive sense of emotional wellbeing.

Therefore providing ways for all 2-year-olds to celebrate all that their bodies can do, to enjoy being as dexterous and as agile as they can, is important. This means ensuring girls and boys, those with highly developed physical skills and those with physical disabilities, are well planned for.

Another challenge of providing this kind of physical play is discussed by LeVoguer and Pasch (2014). This concerns the fears that practitioners have with regards to close physical contact with children, which focus on issues of safeguarding and child protection. However, although protecting children from abuse should always be a priority, these fears can lead to practices that are in themselves detrimental. Goddard-Blythe (2004) claims that responses to these concerns such as no touching policies deprive children of the experience of normal healthy physical holding against which they would otherwise be able to measure abusive touch. Tobin (2004) argues further that seeing all early years practitioners as potential child abusers and young children as vulnerable victims means that the quality and enjoyment of care for children and for early years practitioners are diminished. Citing both these writers, Pound (2013: 42) states that: 'the impact of concerns about holding and touching children limits the effectiveness of professional care and constrains children's development. For young children touch is communication.' With this in mind, we may ask what messages 2-year-olds are receiving if, when they clamber onto a practitioner's lap, they are lifted and down and stood away from them or asked to 'just sit beside me'? These are important issues that need to be discussed as a team and with parents. Practitioners also want to feel protected from allegations but this can only happen when wise but measured policies are agreed and implemented based on sound theory about what young children need rather than on alarmist views and knee-jerk reactions.

The physical environment: balancing the safe with the challenging and dependence with independence

As already stated, a key characteristic of 2-year-olds is their need to balance the desire to explore with the need to feel safe, their independence with their dependence on adults. Creating an environment as 'a third teacher' (Gandini 1998: 177) can support 2-year-olds in succeeding in many of their attempts at independence, thereby enhancing their self-esteem. An effective environment in this regard will have displays, resources and storage areas at appropriate and different levels and plenty of floor-based activities because 2-year-olds often want to squat or lie on their tummies to play. Practitioners experienced in working with 2-year-olds often reduce the number of chairs in the room as children will usually prefer to stand at table top activities. Insisting that a child sits at a table to paint or use cornflour is very likely to deter these very active learners. They need to feel they can easily take off if the activity proves too scary, uninteresting or something more appealing is spotted.

Allowing the 2-year-old to be independent and keep them safe may seem mutually exclusive aims. However, these can both be achieved if held jointly in mind and an environment that is safe, yet offers challenge, is developed. Examples of this include having low balancing beams to walk along, low-growing tree branches to climb and ropes to swing on. The Montessori approach (1919, cited in Pound 2011) has much to teach about how much young child can achieve using real implements if taught the safe technique, for example, with knives, scissors and staplers. If the resources and play opportunities in a setting are too tame, the inventive 2-year-old will find a way to make them more exciting! A child climbing on tables and chairs is a common example of this. But rather than frustratedly (for practitioners and children) repeating 'please get down', practitioners who observe this behaviour will enhance the provision if they ask: 'What challenges are the children looking for and how can I provide this safely?' Creating indoor climbing and raised play areas with stage blocks or similar would safely cater for this, or, if the budget allows, some play equipment manufacturers have two-storey home corners.

The 2-year-old's need for security and continuity is also provided for if much of the room is set out in areas that stay the same, as well as having new resources and activities that provide exciting opportunities for exploration. Think of how bewildering it can be to find your local supermarket has moved the merchandise you seek. Being able to find the resources that they want will help the 2-year-old to feel in control and their play may then be more complex and sustained. Consistent provision also enables repetition; if the blocks only appear twice a week, a 2-year-old's play may get stuck at the exploration stage, that is, finding out what these resources do, and not move on to be incorporated into imaginative play. So opportunities to repeat, practise and master new skills enhance learning as well as raise children's self-confidence.

Outdoors and outings: are 2-year-olds getting out enough?

Margaret McMillan (1860–1931), a pioneer of nursery education at the beginning of the twentieth century, argued that:

> Children want space at all ages, but from age one to seven, that is ample space, wanted almost as much as food and air. To move, to run, to find things out by new movement, to feel one's life in every limb, that is the life of early childhood. And yet one sees dim houses behind whose windows and doors thirty or forty little ones are penned in Day Nurseries.
>
> (reported by Curtis 1950, cited in Goddard Blythe 2004: 173)

It is necessary to ask ourselves whether we are in danger of replicating today this kind of provision with little outdoor space that McMillan was criticizing. UK government regulations state that: 'Providers must provide access to an outdoor play area or, if that is not possible, ensure that outdoor activities are planned and taken on a daily basis' (DFE 2014a: 28). This may be a nod towards the importance of adequate outdoor provision but it remains that large new nurseries are currently being opened in response to the need for day care, which are not required to have their own outdoor play space. Neither are adequate access and child:space ratios laid down (DFE 2014a). This gives a clear message that movement play and play outdoors are seen as not essential.

However, the outdoors is well established as a rich learning environment (McMillan, cited in Ouvry 2003; Tovey 2007) yet practitioners still have to explain to more sceptical colleagues or to worried parents (like Shannon's), and perhaps to managers or proprietors, what the outdoors offers the 2-year-old that indoors cannot. Greenman and Stonehouse (1996: 223–4) explain that this is where young children can experience:

- 'Climate' – the warmth of sun, the chill and sensation of wind and wetness of rain and snow on skin
- 'Landscape' – slopes to walk up and roll down, stony paths to balance on, streams to venture into or over, as well as the variety of colour and textures
- 'Openness' – the height of the sky and, if not too fenced in, the land where running, swinging, spinning, kicking and throwing unfettered are possible
- 'Messiness' – for mud play, large brush mark making on walls and ground with paint or water, and with chalks
- 'Wildlife' – worms, birds and insects to encounter, all in their natural environment rather than caged, where there is the burden of care, which deters some settings from having pets
- 'People' – ordinary people going about their day-to-day activities.

This list of experiences will contribute well to the richness of experience that a nursery garden might offer. However, to ensure young children's experiences extend beyond this and also so they feel they are part of society, they need to go out into the community. Here they can be part of normal life in the streets, where they can see people out jogging, walking with a stick, some shopping, others digging up roads, dogs out for a walk and cats strolling on walls, cars with four wheels or great lorries with eight. Nursery-bound children miss out on a wealth of experiences and on a sense of belonging to their community; equally, the community misses out on seeing its children out and about being part of everyday life.

However, for some settings, such outings may pose a problem in meeting adult:child ratios, but if being part of the community is truly valued, then ways can be found; volunteers, students and parents can be drawn on to help. The success of any outing with 2-year-olds is dependent on how well matched it is to the characteristics of this age group (Manning-Morton and Thorp 2003). Their 'in the moment' perspective of life and limited verbal language mean that they will get the most out of being part of very small groups with people they know well. As the size of the group increases so does the amount of organization and the need to exercise control. Consequently the freedom for children to walk on walls, for example, or to change the original route in order to follow a child's interest, will decrease. Effective outings build on children's immediate experiences and reflect normal life, such as going on practical errands. Here is one such that Shannon, Alexio and Angelina were part of:

Case study

Kirsty had arranged for a family pet to visit the group and the visiting puppy had done a wee on the rug. Kirsty and a student took Shannon, Alexio and Angelina and one other child to the launderette to wash it. The children helped choose a trolley from the garden that the rug would fit into and they all pulled it there together. They helped load and feed money into the washing machine and went to the park nearby while it washed. The most memorable part was trying to pull the heavy wet rug back and running after the trolley when it rolled down a slope without them. Photos were taken and great enjoyment was had looking at these later and telling the group and the children's parents all about it.

Conclusion

Two-year-olds in group settings generally thrive, learn and experience a sense of well-being when their physicality is recognized, appreciated and planned for. This of course needs to be coupled with the secure base provided by an attuned Key Person relationship that provides the confidence to take risks. The exuberance and enjoyment of gaining increasing control and enjoying and celebrating what their body can do when this provision is in place may go some way to set the direction for future development and all-round well-being. After all, this is in an era where concerns about poor health, obesity and lack of exercise in older children and adults are rife. However, opportunities for young children to be climbing, pulling, pushing, transporting and being as independent and active as possible will not be embedded in practice or survive opposition from the less well-informed unless practitioners have opportunities to discuss practice, evaluate and review policies. They also need to have access to ongoing training to learn about new thinking about child development and to incorporate this into practice.

8　New territories of knowledge and understanding

Introduction

Journeys that are interesting and exciting are not just concerned with getting from A to B; they are about understanding the whole area, making connections between places and discovering different routes. So it is with 2-year-olds' journeys in thinking and making sense. They are piecing together the different parts of the terrain they are covering, which creates a unique map in their minds. This chapter discusses some of the key perceptual, cognitive and creative skills that 2-year-olds are using to develop their map.

This chapter also explores how developing cognitive understanding in the third year of life is characterized by the changeability that is suggested by the theory of reciprocal interweaving (Gesell 1952, cited in Piek 2006), as discussed in the introduction to this book. There are times when a 2-year-old will appear wise beyond their years, yet others when they misunderstand something that seems obvious. They can appear fearless in their approach to the world yet also develop fears which seem inexplicable to an adult (Miller 2004). The rapidity of cognitive development at this point in life means that 2-year-olds can feel overwhelmed by the huge amount of new information and experiences in their lives. This means they can find life exciting and scary, interesting and confusing, satisfying and frustrating in equal measure. These features of a 2-year-old's experience of life have implications for how practitioners provide for their play and learning; the aim is to provide balance in practice and provision so that the children can find equilibrium.

This is also important in the psychological environment that the practitioner creates. A 2-year-old's exploration of the world is not confined to objects and the physical environment; it also embraces emotional and social relationships with friends and adults and the understanding of self that these relationships provide. It is the security and trust in these relationships that support 2-year-olds in their confident exploration of new territories of knowledge, so the role of the practitioner as a fellow traveller in the world of ideas and as a 'base-camp' for their explorations is also discussed here.

Case studies

One of Lewis's (2y7m) important 'people' is his family dog and part of his daily routine is to take the dog for a walk with his Dad, Steve. Steve says that their walk has to follow the same route though and Lewis always has to walk along the front walls of the houses on his street. Lewis loves to join in with any household activity that matches his interests, imitating how his Dad does things. So he holds the dog's lead wrapped around his hand like Steve and lines up the tins in the cupboard after shopping just like him too. Sweeping and vacuuming are favourite activities, in fact, Steve says that their vacuum cleaner is frequently brought out at home for play rather than cleaning!

At his childminder's Lewis is 'into everything', particularly water, so Chantal, his childminder, has set up a piece of guttering in the garden, down which he loves to shoot water and balls. Chantal says he has recently been interested in throwing, catching and kicking large balls but can get a bit frustrated at missing them. She adds that at the park recently, Lewis repeatedly climbed the steps to the slide and back down again instead of going down the slide, all the while repeating 'up 'n' down, up 'n' down' to himself. His current favourite story is *Harvey Slumpfenberger's Christmas Present* (Burningham 2000). He has started to re-enact this by putting a block 'present' in the truck and riding it to the shed in the garden. Chantal set up a doll's bed and doll at the end of the garden so he could deliver the 'present'.

* * *

Kwan (2y0m) is sometimes overwhelmed by strong emotions, particularly when there is change, so it is very important to her that things stay the same. For example, she always checks that her coat is still on her peg since Jane put Randy's coat there by mistake. This was confusing because Randy has the same coat and Kwan was upset when she thought Randy might be wearing hers. For a while she would repeatedly say 'Randy got my coat' and needed Jane to repeat the mantra, 'This is Kwan's coat, the one with the pink label inside, Randy's coat doesn't have a pink label' and Kwan would repeat, 'Randy no label', shaking her head.

'Again, again' is Kwan's favourite phrase at key group time, requesting that Jane repeatedly reads her favourite story *The Gruffalo* (Donaldson 1999), insisting that every word is read exactly as it is written and that they repeat the same actions at the same point in the story each time. When Jane was away and Helen read the story, Kwan would shout 'No, no' each time Helen read a phrase differently or left an action out.

On Thursday mornings, Kwan's key group go to the library and then come back for lunch but the library changed the story session to the afternoon. She got very confused and frustrated that it was time to go home when they returned and kept asking about having pudding. When her parent tried to get her to put her coat on to leave, she refused and ran off to hide by wrapping herself in the curtain, where she was found sucking her thumb and clutching her Ted-ted.

As well as Ted-ted, Kwan has a collection of soft toys and dolls at home, which she keeps on her bed, each wrapped in their own blanket or piece of cloth. If her Mum changes this whilst tidying up, she has to re-order them before bed-time and she then covers all of them with the end of her duvet. Last week Kwan's Mum made the mistake of washing the dolls' blankets as they had juice spilled on them. Kwan has complained ever since that they have 'gone funny'. It took her Mum a while to realize that this meant that they now smelled of the new fabric softener she had used.

Taking in the surroundings: 2-year-olds still learning through their senses

A 2-year-old's understanding of the world is mediated predominantly through their senses and movement. For some children, sensory information may sometimes even be processed cross-modally in the brain, thereby 'hearing colours' or 'seeing sounds', for example (Carter 1998: 22) and of course, young children with perhaps a sight or hearing impairment will develop the ability to hear or smell more acutely. Although this kind of perceptual development may be limited to a few children, all 2-year-olds' senses are very sensitive and so they can be affected by noises, smells and flavours more intensely than most adults. This is particularly the case with their senses of smell and hearing, which, mature since birth, continue to give them huge amounts of information (like Kwan's understanding of her dolls' blankets), while their vision, always less mature than the other senses in the early years, continues to develop (Berk 2009).

Perceptual development

Perception is the processing of sensory information and is fundamental to brain and cognitive development. This includes the overall senses of sight, hearing, smell, taste, touch, proprioception and kinaesthesia as well as the more detailed aspects of each of them such as depth perception. Rita Carter (1998) describes how the sense organs – the ears, nose, eyes, mouth and skin – gather sensory information, which then enters the brain as a series of electrical pulses. The brain modifies and sorts this information by processing it through neural pathways to specific areas of the brain and thereby translates it into visual, aural or other sensations.

But young children do not only take in sensory information; they also transform and rearrange it in their minds. Indeed, as Carter (1998) points out, we can never perceive the same thing in the same way twice because the sensory impact of something alters our subsequent perception of it, which in turn creates an altered impact, which further alters our perception . . . and so on.

A relevant feature of visual development in 2-year-olds is the now greater sensitivity in the marginal areas of their vision, which may be related to their tendency to be easily distracted. In addition, their increasing visual range means they can spot familiar objects a long way off, which may inspire them to move off and explore away from the immediate activity. But their vision is still immature in other ways. For example, some spatial understanding, such as judging distances and differentiating between near and far, is still developing and may result in misjudging where to place themselves in relation to something or someone else (Ames and Ilg 1976). For example, in the case study above, by building on Lewis's interest and providing opportunities for throwing, catching and kicking balls, Chantal was using a simple game to effectively aid his perceptual skills. The physical movement involved would help Lewis to see things from different perspectives and increase his understanding of spatial concepts. Another visual challenge for 2-year-olds is that they may find it hard to find something with their eyes again after having looked away from it. So being expected to understand objects through vision alone is inappropriate; 2-year-olds need to touch and hold objects in order to understand them well.

Manipulating objects, moving them around, taking them apart and putting them together with other objects are therefore very important actions. These behaviours lead to understanding how different parts of objects work, the effect objects have on each other and, very importantly, the effects the child's actions have on the object. Such investigations are central to a 2-year-old's major research project into life, the universe and everything. In this way, information about the world pours in through the 2-year-old's eyes, nose, mouth, skin and ears. They store, remember and use this information to understand, make meaning and plan future actions. It is their maturing perceptual abilities, their well-developed physical skills and abiding interest in moving around that underpin their cognitive skills.

Making maps of new terrain: representation and memory

Two-year-olds are (and have been since birth) using their perceptual categorizations to create representations in their minds. In this context representation means knowledge or the way in which humans store information. Jean Mandler (cited in Goswami 1998) suggests that perception becomes meaning-based knowledge through the child's physical experience of the spatial properties of objects and events. They recognize what is similar about the movements and spatial relations of these events and categorize them by creating an 'image-schema' (cited in Goswami 1998: 54). This process of forming mental representations is central to cognition.

Perspectives on cognitive development

Piaget (1896–1980)

Piaget's idea of cognitive development is that it occurs in stages that are universal and invariant, each of which is qualitatively different in its cognitive structures and modes of thought. He describes that during the sensory motor period babies and toddlers build on their reflex actions through active exploration, thereby developing mental operations he called schemas. They assimilate new experiences into their existing schemes of thought and thereby adjust or accommodate concepts and develop more complex schemas. The motivation for adjusting and adapting to the environment in this way is the discomfort of what he called disequilibrium, and to maintain a state of equilibrium, which Piaget described as the preferred, more comfortable state (Piaget and Inhelder 1969).

Information Processing Approach

In contrast, an Information Processing Approach suggests that cognitive understanding happens by taking in more and more information and thereby creating more complex representations (Berk 2009). As more information is processed in the brain, each piece of information is linked with other pieces of information and stored in memory.

Representational re-description

Annette Karmiloff-Smith (1992, 1995) proposes a view of cognitive development that also focusses on the ability to store, retrieve and use representations in memory. But her theory of representational re-description

---

also describes qualitative differences between different levels of re-description. She aims to explain how children's representations become more flexible as repeated experience leads to multiple representations, re-described each time and stored at different levels in the mind.

As well as forming representations of objects and experiences, we need to be able to store information anvd retrieve it. So memory is crucial to being able to use mental representations in learning. For example, Lewis's representations of using balls in different ways will be stored and retrieved each time he plays, gradually making his representations more complex, until one day he may be able to juggle!

Two-year-olds often show that they have very good memories for events, which are often triggered by similar sensory information that might have gone unnoticed by the adult. So when the child makes a connection in their mind between two experiences or objects, which may seem obscure or outlandish, the adult's task is to keep an open mind and explore a little further in order to understand what the connection might be, rather than dismiss it out of hand. For example, when Lewis saw a white horse in a story he kept saying 'It Father Christmas.' Chantal immediately knew that in his favourite book, Father Christmas rides on a white horse at one point, so she was able to recall other aspects of the story with him and make links to his play and to previous experiences such as the horses at the city farm and that the Father Christmas they saw in the market had a reindeer not a horse. In this way the adult provides the child with a conceptual framework and a supplementary memory bank to contextualize their thinking.

Making sense of time and space

The kinds of shared discussions and explorations described above are valuable in supporting a 2-year-old's developing understanding of concepts of time and space and the appearance and existence of objects (including people).

A 2-year-old is still heavily dependent on the external appearance of things for their understanding of what they are and how they might behave, reflecting their still limited experience of the world (Goswami 1998). This can be seen in the way they will expect something that looks like a sweet to be a sweet, not a medicine or a washing machine tablet, which can result in many everyday misunderstandings as well as in potentially dangerous scenarios as in this example. This still immature ability to differentiate between the appearance and the reality of an object is linked to their emergent ability to take others' perspectives and understand their minds, as discussed in Chapter 4. It is also linked to their limited understanding of 'conservation' (Piaget 1952b) of quantity, number and mass, resulting, for example, in arguments about having the 'big' (tall) cup even though the 'small' cup holds the same amount of juice because it is wider as well as shorter than the other cup.

But the foundations of these yet to mature understandings have been laid through their previously established understanding of the constancy of objects' size, shape, colour and other properties. This understanding has been gained through constant physical exploration and manipulation of a wide range of things and their experience of many events. Continued and repeated opportunities to explore in this way build on the foundations of that previous experience. For example, in the case study we can see Lewis learning about concepts of space through going up and down the slide steps. Two-year-olds learn about in and out, in front and behind, on and under by putting their bodies in these positions and then, like Lewis saying 'up 'n' down', will use many different words relating to space such as there, where, go away, turn around. Older 2-year-olds with their more refined sense of space may also use concepts of 'near' and 'far away' and ask abstract questions in relation to space such as 'where do spiders live?', concepts that will be influenced by the child's socio-cultural experience. This conceptual understanding may be observed in their insistence that things are put precisely where they think they should go, as in the case study of Kwan's ordering of her dolls and hanging her coat on her peg.

Unlike spatial concepts, concepts of time are not understood so easily through physical exploration, so a key characteristic of 2-year-olds is that they still very much live in the present. They don't quite have the same approach to getting things done or reaching a destination that an adult has, getting caught up in what is happening in the moment, like Lewis walking on the walls and completely forgetting that they were walking the dog to the vets.

However, a 2-year-old's more sophisticated understanding of object permanency means they are perhaps not so much 'in the here and now' as a toddler (Stonehouse 1990; Manning-Morton and Thorp 2003, 2006). This means they can readily grasp sequence, so giving an explanation to Kwan in the case study of 'today we are going to the library after lunch and then it will be time to go home' would have helped her to more easily accept the change. Older 2-year-olds can often explain a sequence of events themselves and can also conceive of divisions of time such as 'morning' and 'afternoon', although 'last night' could refer to an event a week ago as well as yesterday.

This emergent understanding of time is most effectively supported through providing the concrete experience of a predictable flow to the routine of the day, reinforced by many visual and aural cues such as picture timetables, like the one Kwan's Key Person developed following her confusion about the library visit times. By providing consistency and continuity of experience in routines the practitioner enables the child to use their memory to make connections in their thinking about events, using their shared repeated experiences to remind them of what has occurred previously and so what might happen in the future, thereby acting like an external clock or shared calendar on a computer network.

These aspects of a 2-year-old's cognitive journey mean that effective 'sustained shared thinking' (Sylva et al. 2004) with 2-year-olds has an additional facet. Sustained shared thinking involves the mutual effort of interested children and adults in developing new understanding. Sylva et al. (2004: 6) define it as: 'an episode in which two or more individuals "work together" in an intellectual way to solve a problem, clarify a concept, evaluate activities'. However, given the understanding of time and space that 2-year-olds are developing, sustained shared thinking also means ensuring there is continuity of thought between events so that thinking is sustained over time; this relies on a good level of consistency of Key Person interaction and consistency of peer group, both of which are harder to maintain when there are a lot of children attending a setting part-time.

Flights of imagination: symbolic representation and creativity

As well as knowledge, or ways of storing information, the term representation is also used to mean the use of symbols to denote experience (Schaffer 2006). Piaget (1962) suggested that children do not start to use symbolic representation until the end of the sensori-motor period. But the beginning of children's use of symbols is seen in their first gestures, such as declarative pointing, signs and words. Then, as they use everyday objects in recreated scenarios such as talking on the telephone, their use of imagination begins to take off. Soon they begin to use objects that are unrelated to the real thing, such as Lewis using a block to be a present. Using abstract symbols such as this is usually thought of as only emerging at about 3 years old (Piaget 1962; Vygotsky 1966). However, many experienced practitioners observe this happening earlier (Manning-Morton and Thorp 2003, 2006).

Imitation is an important part of the process of developing representations. Piaget (1962) suggested that imitation and the creation of internal mental images are the first step towards symbolic representation and we can see 2-year-olds practising this step as they imitate familiar domestic scenarios and then recreate them in their play, as Lewis does in the case study. This is why it is important to ensure that 2-year-olds have many opportunities to be involved in the real tasks of the domestic life of their early childhood setting as well as their homes. Another important element of practice is the focused engagement and participation by practitioners in the imaginative play of 2-year-olds. Slade (1987) found that the length of episodes of symbolic/pretend play and the complexity of this play are greater when mothers are available to play with their 12- to 24-month-old children and also when they model this type of play. This aspect of being an active play partner is something that practitioners who are used to working with older children often note as a key difference when working with 2-year-olds. But by modelling and supporting symbolic and imaginative play, practitioners are contributing more to 2-year-olds' thinking than if they sit them in groups to name flashcards, for example, because imaginative people are great thinkers, inventors and problem solvers. These are key learning skills.

For this reason, seeing creativity and imagination as limited to producing paintings or as only the prerogative of older children or artistic adults is short-sighted and results in the inherent creativity of all children being overlooked (Manning-Morton and Thorp 2003, 2006). Two-year-olds express themselves creatively in all sorts of ways but reproducing, for example, an adult's idea of a Christmas tree is not one of them. This kind of activity, so often seen in settings, is more appropriate to preparing someone to work on factory assembly lines than supporting young children's creativity (Thorp 2003). A more relevant experience would be exploring pine branches, which would match most 2-year-olds' fascination with the natural world and prompt scientific exploration as well as link creative expression and spiritual experience.

Children's interest in representation through mark making is often first apparent when babies use a side-to-side arm motion and find that they have made arc patterns in spilled food (Matthews 2003). This fascination in leaving their mark continues and can be encouraged through making available paint, flour and a wealth of other materials to experiment with and a range of tools to make marks with, including their own bodies. By 2 years old children's current schemas may be evident in their mark making as they bang the crayon all over the paper, or sweep a paint brush up and down or in circular motions (Matthews 2003). This is the beginning of representational drawing; they are representing the movements they are interested in and may even describe splodges of paint as 'doing a frog'. This is the foundation that underpins later recognizable representations of people, vehicles and so on. This progression is undermined by practitioners imposing unnecessary rules or having unrealistic expectations of the 2-year-old, such as 'what is that?' questions, and comments such as 'draw nicely' in response to vigorous dotting or 'fill up the rest of the paper'. However, practitioners who show their interest by commenting on the whirling lines or use of colour will encourage the 2-year-old artist. Older 2-year-olds may ask adults to draw for them. This can provide them with something so far removed from what they can attain that it discourages their attempts. However, adopting a totally hands-off approach appears as disinterest or being unwilling to help. Instead, drawing together is preferable, talking about the shapes in what they want to draw, the colours they want to use and making connections with shapes or strokes they have used before. It is important not to give the impression that drawing, painting and making are just something to entertain children. Drawing children's attention to illustrations in stories, patterns on fabrics and out in the community on buildings will help children recognize that they are part of a society that creates.

Making connections: schemas

As identified above, a key feature of the representations of 2-year-olds is that they often recreate an experience through action. Such re-enactments will include repeated patterns of movement such as throwing, spinning or carrying objects from one place to another. Valuing and providing for this dynamic aspect of children's schemas (Athey 2003) are essential in provision for 2-year-olds. This means practitioners need to understand that children who appear to be flitting from one activity to another may in fact be exploring a particular idea or concept in some depth. Also, behaviours that may appear anti-social, such as throwing, can in fact indicate a child's schematic preoccupations. The practitioner can then understand the child better and provide appropriate play opportunities and environments that support the child's explorations in a positive way (Manning-Morton and Thorp 2003, 2006).

Reflective exercise

Review the case studies at the beginning of this chapter. Which different schematic interests can you identify in Lewis's and Kwan's behaviours?

You may have identified Lewis's interest in trajectory (throwing, going up and down the slide, pulling the hoover) and that this may be linked to an interest in positioning (placing and ordering items in a particular way, such as lining up the tins, walking along the walls). Kwan also has an interest in where things are but most obviously is exploring an enveloping schema (wrapping up her dolls in their blankets and herself in the curtain).

These are examples of schemas commonly seen in 2-year-olds, as are:

- Connection: joining resources together, connecting things together with string or tape, for example
- Enclosure: filling and emptying containers, building walls around things or self
- Rotation: spinning around, fascination with wheels, spinning washing machines
- Transforming: interest in mixing materials together such as mud and water or how materials change such as ice and water
- Transporting: carrying objects in bags, buggies, trucks, etc. from one place to another.

(Manning-Morton and Thorp 2006)

***

Schemas

Schemas are repeated and coordinated patterns of movement and perception that become mental constructs or concepts. As toddlers and 2-year-olds build on their earlier sensory experiences by repeating actions in different contexts, their existing schemas become more complex (Piaget 1962). In this way children form higher level and more powerful schemas, using them to organize their knowledge and understanding. As children's schemas become coordinated, we are able to observe that they develop in clusters (Nutbrown 1999; Bruce 2001; Athey 2003).

Children show their schemas dynamically through movements and actions such as dancing round, climbing up or crawling into, and configuratively in their drawings, paintings and models, such as building a high tower or painting around the edge of the paper.

Children use schemas at four levels (Athey 2003):

- 'Motor': through their senses, actions and movements
- 'Symbolic representation': when they make something stand for something else
- 'Functional dependency': when they understand and explore cause and effect
- 'Thought': when they talk about their schematic play.

***

Providing a secure base for 2-year-olds' learning adventures

A 2-year-old's journey in thinking and making sense can have both smooth, easy paths with clear signposts and bumpy stretches with hurdles put in the way. Much of that which either facilitates or impedes their progress comes from the adults who care for them. Therefore practitioners need to consider how they provide a facilitating psychological environment for 2-year-olds' learning. Key to this is providing children with a secure base of a trusting, warm relationship with a Key Person from whom a 2-year-old can confidently go out and explore the physical world and the world of ideas and retreat to when the wider world feels too much.

Secure base

'Secure base' describes the ambience created by the attachment figure within which a child can integrate the excitement of exploring away from the carer with the feeling of safety in the carer's presence (Ainsworth 1982, cited in Holmes 2014: 70). How to do this is a central developmental focus for 2-year-olds and can be observed through specific behaviours which enable practitioners to understand how much independence or close contact the child wants or needs at any given time, for example, seeking the carer out or walking away, sitting near or hiding, clinging or running off send different messages. How a 2-year-old learns to integrate these opposing needs relates to their ability to balance autonomy with intimacy and individual fulfilment with social belonging throughout their lives.

This aspect of the Key Person's role requires the practitioner to be 'tuned in' to when a child needs or wants a practitioner to be involved in their play and if so, in what way. Practitioners need to be both supportive of children's moves to independence but still accepting of their need for dependence. For example, it is often tempting to move away from an activity once children are 'settled' but for 2-year-olds this can be very disruptive so practitioners need to be sensitive to when their presence and involvement in play are necessary.

The Key Person also needs to be attuned to different responses in children, for example, when an imaginative game or story is tipping over from the thrill of the unknown or slightly scary to overwhelming confusion and fear for a particular child. As discussed earlier, the 2-year-old's cognitive journey sees them veer between two poles: one being the security of concrete, known experiences and the other the exhilaration of taking off on a 'flight of imagination'. This requires thoughtfully developed provision that is responsive to these fluctuations. Ensuring that there are a good number of real objects such as bowls, spoons or phones but also open-ended materials such as lengths of cloth that can be used in whatever way a child chooses, means that each child can find their own balance between reality and imagination. In addition, balancing new and exciting play opportunities and materials with familiar ones helps a 2-year-old to feel confident in their explorations and to avoid feeling overwhelmed by a constant flow of new information.

The effectiveness of the secure base that the Key Person provides is also founded on how well they know each key child. It is particularly useful to know their fears, habits and current concerns. Sometimes quite ordinary things such as vacuum cleaners can be linked in a child's mind with something scary, giving rise to what may seem like irrational fears to adults (see Miller 1992: 43). This arises from the rapid changes in 2-year-olds' cognitive understanding and making connections between their experiences, which sometimes leads to forming a slightly wrong idea about something: yes, vacuum cleaners suck things up; no, they do not suck up children! It is very complicated for a young child to be able to learn about things that adults take for granted as a daily reality so 2-year-olds often have routines or rituals that give them some measure of control over their immediate world and help them to manage scary situations, such as Kwan's fixation on her coat. These rituals need to be honoured and fears met with sympathy and understanding rather than being dismissed or minimized.

There are also many concepts in a 2-year-old's social and family life which they cannot hope to grasp fully but which their caring adults need to be able to talk to them about with explanations that are within their current grasp and with the full knowledge that the topic will need to be revisited over years to come. Issues such as divorce, the death of a grandparent or pet, being adopted, having same sex parents or a single parent all need to be broached in simple, straightforward terms and in a way that is not going to increase the child's anxiety or emotional burden. Following up such conversations by providing relevant play materials and opportunities will support the child in expressing, re-creating and 'playing out' their ideas about these situations. This may include particular props but materials such as paint or clay or reading books and telling stories are also very useful. Two-year-olds use fantasy to protect themselves psychically from scary events, so their stories are often full of terrible things happening to others; listening to their stories can support them in managing their fears and also give interesting insights into their fantasy life.

Conclusion

Our greater awareness of rapid growth in neural connections in the first three years of life and 2-year-olds' huge capacity for learning have led to ideas that if children don't have 'enriched' experiences and learn things early, then it will be too late for them to catch up. This sometimes results in immersing very young children in focused 'learning' experiences: learning experiences that are often misguided and even detrimental to 2-year-olds' positive dispositions.

Such 'hot-housing' of young children is often based on hearsay rather than an informed understanding of brain development (Bruer 1997). Wolfe and Brandt (1998) suggest four key findings which they believe are 'well established' about brain development: that the brain changes physiologically as a result of experience; that IQ is not fixed at birth; that some abilities are acquired more easily during certain sensitive periods; and that learning is strongly affected by emotion. Therefore, Gopnik et al. (1999) identify that a 'rich' environment for very young children comprises everyday domestic activities with conversation and involvement in the regular daily routines of the home or setting and outings into the community, in the context of responsive, consistent close relationships. This, they say, will provide just the right amount of stimulation for good synaptic genesis and pruning.

As a 2-year-old's explorations broaden, their understanding of how the world works expands at a rapid rate. They are fascinated by the effect of their actions on objects and substances and need to repeat their experiments again and again to see if the effect or result is the same or different. They need to be able to carry out these experiments in contexts of social and emotional meaning and security.

9 Following different paths: planning with 2-year-olds

Introduction

One of the principles that underpin the Early Years Foundation Stage (EYFS) that guides early years provision in England is 'The Unique Child' (DFE 2014a). It is easy to pay lip service to this principle but to take it seriously means that practitioners need to know each child really well when planning for their possible learning journeys. This includes knowing their level of development and potential development, their cultural and family backgrounds, their interests and their fears. No wonder that the guidance for Scottish provision states that in planning and providing for young children practitioners must 'think first about children as individuals and what is best for them' (Learning and Teaching Scotland 2010: 20).

This chapter examines these and other principles that guide the practice of planning provision for 2-year-olds, including the principles that all planning should be based on regular and frequent observation of children and that practice and provision should be reviewed and evaluated regularly. Practical ways of approaching this task are also suggested, which hopefully would take practitioners away from being with the children for as little time as possible.

Observing each 2-year-old's journey – a waste of time or a pleasure?

Some practitioners when asked what they enjoy about working with 2-year-olds will describe how rewarding it is to see how rapidly they develop, examples of children's rapid language development or their incredible physical or problem-solving skills are often given. These amazing and distinctive journeys can be captured and celebrated through observation, which can then inform the planning of further excursions into the 2-year-old's particular areas of interest. However, for this to be effective, the observations need to be of sufficient quality. Poor observation that is regarded more as a chore or a duty has scant impact on enhancing children's experiences, yields little enjoyment for practitioners or parents but still takes time away from interacting with the children. This state of affairs is exacerbated if practitioners have a large number of key children (as currently generated by the UK government targets for increased numbers of funded part-time places for 2-year-olds; DfE 2011), little time to sit and observe, and limited opportunities for reflection and discussion of their findings.

Some settings ensure that practitioners record child observations by setting targets. However, this can result in the majority being short, 'snapshot' observations written to identify the 'Development Matters' progressive steps listed under each of the Areas of Learning set out in this curriculum guidance (BAECE 2012). Although such notes can capture a significant new development like 'holds pencil between thumb and two fingers' (BAECE 2012: 24), they cannot give the kind of holistic view of a child that is necessary to really understand the 'Unique Child'. Adopting a holistic approach means thinking about children and their experiences in an integrated way rather than dividing the focus into different areas. This kind of integrated thinking is effectively developed through undertaking holistic observations which include both the context and the social and emotional content of a scenario. Two methods of observing and recording in this way are The Infant Observation Technique (Miller et al. 1989; Elfer, cited in Abbot and Langston 2005) and Learning Stories (Carr and Lee 2012).

Infant Observation Technique (Miller et al. 1989)

These observations are undertaken by psychotherapy students as part of their training. The student observes a child weekly for a period of a year, either at home or in an early years setting. Unlike observations done by practitioners in early years settings, the observer does not take any notes during the hour-long visit. Instead they are simply 'there', taking in everything that they see. Then, as soon as possible afterwards, the observer writes up their observation in as much detail as possible. It might be thought that important detail is lost this way, but what is retained are the observer's feelings about what is observed as well as the incidents that resonate most in the observer's mind. These are then explored in a weekly seminar group, which helps the observer to understand what they have observed and not to become too overwhelmed by any feelings provoked during the visit, because the group 'contains' the observer's emotional response, a practice that could usefully be adapted for use in early years settings (Miller et al. 1989, cited in Manning-Morton 2011).

This technique provides a wealth of detail about the child and their experience because the observer notices every small example of a look, an expression, interaction or body language. It also highlights the emotional 'temperature' of the environment through reflecting on the observer's own emotional responses to what they see. This is in stark contrast to the usual notion of 'objectivity' in observation, whereby the observer's emotional responses may be present but not recorded or explored. However, by making them explicit, the adult's feelings can be discussed and used to think about the child's emotional world. This approach also gives the written observation a different tone. Elfer (2005) compares how practitioners *speak* with warmth and enthusiasm about what they see their key children doing and yet they *write* observations in a rather stiff, clinical way. The paradox is that to be valuable, observations need to be factual and without bias yet convey the qualitative atmosphere of a scenario which has emotional content. Therefore the recorded information must be both appropriate to what is being observed and use language that conveys the context and the quality of what was observed.

Reflective exercise

Compare these observations:

Hanna (2y5m) is playing at the water play tray, standing up. One other child is present. Hanna looks at him. She lifts up her left arm and shakes the ball that she has found in the water, holding it in a pincer grip. She passes it to her right hand and using a palmer grasp she drops it into the water. She looks at the water splashing. Then she pulls at her wet tee shirt with finger and thumb and walks away. (3 min)

Hanna (2y5m) follows, watches and then copies Ben (2y0m). She reaches into the water tray and picks out a ball as he has. They look at each other and laugh. She looks at the water dripping from her hand, frowning, and lifts it up high away from the water. She shakes it but the water just runs down her arm. She quickly swaps hands and then drops the ball into the water. The resulting splash seems to interest both children until Hanna looks down at the wet patches the splash made on her tee shirt. Frowning more deeply and pulling at her tee shirt she walks away. Only three minutes have elapsed.

If using the Infant Observation Technique the observer would have recorded this straight after, not during the event and they may have included: 'When she quickly swapped hands and dropped the ball, I wondered what she was thinking and when she pulled at her tee shirt and walked away, I was both disappointed that she hadn't been able to continue her interest in the water and friendship with Ben and frustrated that no-one noticed her difficulty.'

The first observation is factual; it describes the scene and is in the present tense making it clear and immediate, and contains no judgemental language. However, the observer seems to be focussing on the physical development of Hanna, identifying aspects such as 'pincer grip' that offer nothing new or interesting (as this is usually well established by 2y5m). There is little to learn about Hanna here or to inform planning.

However, the second observation could lead to noting her emerging strategies in making friends (i.e. observing, imitating) and reflection on other signs of interest she shows in others and how to support this. The inclusion of some reflection on the observer's own emotional responses to the scenario gave some insight into Hanna's feelings about the situation and about possible practice issues. Practitioners might ponder on whether Hanna is currently rather worried about getting wet, and why this might be. This may mean that she is not able to enjoy the opportunities water play provides. They might wonder whether this extends to paint and gluing, so follow up with an observation of this. Interesting discussions of ways to support Hanna in her explorations can then be held between the Key Person, colleagues and Hanna's parents. What messages is Hanna receiving about getting wet or messy?

We can see then that the way observations are written and their tone can make a big difference to how valuable they are. This is also the case when using a Learning Story approach (Carr and Lee 2012).

Learning Stories

A Learning Story is a format used to document a child's learning. It was developed by Margaret Carr and colleagues in New Zealand and is widely used there and in Australia, and increasingly, in the UK and Ireland. It uses 'story telling' to describe a child's learning process, focusing primarily on children's dispositions and approaches to learning. A Learning Story starts with noticing something a child has initiated or responded to in their own particular way; this is the 'Initiative' aspect. It then describes how the experience or event unfolds, how the child interacts with others, objects and materials during the experience, their conversations and levels of interest and so on. These are the 'Engagement', 'Intentionality' and 'Relationships' aspects.

Learning Stories focus on positive aspects – what the child can do rather than what the child cannot do – and tell the story of this experience or event directly to the child, to the family, to the practitioner and to others.

Unlike observations such as running and anecdotal records, Learning Stories often use direct speech in the way they are written, as in the following example, 'The wrong shoes', about Reece (2y8m):

Case study

When I entered the room you were looking through the window into the outdoor area. I felt happy when you turned and saw me, because you came with a big smile and took my hand taking me over to the door. When I asked if you wanted to go outside you said, 'Out . . . bike.' I looked down at your feet and said, 'Shoes?' 'Yeah,' you replied. You picked up Akira's shoes. (I thought they were yours.) You did really well getting them on. I started to laugh when I found out they were not your shoes as you obviously already knew. You laughed as I said, 'No, these aren't your shoes. These are your shoes.' I handed your shoes to you and helped you take off Akira's. 'One, two,' you said as I showed you your shoes. You then proceeded to put Akira's back on. You were smiling; I think you must have liked Akira's shoes. 'Sorry,' I said. 'Akira needs his shoes now.' And so we put your shoes on.

Practitioners using this approach report not only that they discover even more wonderful things about the child (such as Reece's understanding of humour) but that using direct speech makes them feel closer to the child and also more ethically accountable for what they write. The observer then writes about 'what does this mean?' and 'what next?', thus using the Learning Story as an assessment tool, interpreting a child's learning dispositions and evaluating and planning further experiences. Learning Stories also strengthen partnership working as the format includes space for the child's, their parents' and colleagues' views too.

Another feature of a Learning Story is the inclusion of photographs and other materials to illustrate the story. Current technology enables practitioners to capture this detail with ease. Of course, issues of privacy must be resolved and child protection safeguards need to be in place, but using photographs and video clips can provide useful material for discussion with children, parents and colleagues. One North London borough has gone further and uses tablet computers in their children's centres. Parents can log on to their child's site, see the clips practitioners have recorded and add comments. This may feel onerous to those not well versed in using recent technology, however, once mastered, practitioners may find it enables even very young children to reflect on what they have achieved and how they have tackled problems. This fosters memory, recall and the development of metacognition (being able to think about how you think) (Robson 2006). It is higher-order thinking like this that helps to develop strategies for learning, to self-assess and to regulate behaviour.

However, using digital technology has its limitations too. Thought needs to be given to the important differences in sensory experience between a screen and a scrapbook-style profile book (Manning-Morton and Thorp 2006). It is not possible, for example, to keep the piece of sheep's wool a child found, attached to a computer, whereas the piece collected by Billie as a young child is still in a pocket in her profile book, which she occasionally still looks at *and* touches *and* smells 18 years later! It is important to remember that such physical sensory experiences also underpin recall and metacognition and are central to 2-year-olds' learning.

Whichever way observations are stored, what is important is to use a variety of observation methods to capture the fullest possible picture of each unique child and to read/watch and ponder over what has been recorded. Files full of unused observations are a waste of time and space. Observation is an invaluable tool and has contributed much to our understanding of young children when used by theorists such as Piaget and Isaacs (Fawcett 2009) and practitioners identify it as a key skill and essential practice as it enables them to: 'enter the child's world' and 'helps people to tune in . . . observing and listening to children to really get to know what they need' (Manning-Morton 2014: 150). In this way, the information captured and shared through observation reaps pleasure and reward for practitioners, parents and children and can inform everyone's understanding. Moreover, observation aids in the assessment of the quality of provision as it illuminates children's actual day-to-day experiences, providing information about children's social interactions with adults and other children, as well as their development and learning (NICH and HD 2006).

Assessments: do they follow each unique child's path or do they lead to dead ends?

Assessment is just one part of a cycle that sits most comfortably between observation and planning. High quality assessment and planning flow from observation and enhance children's day-to-day experience.

On occasions practitioners will encounter 2-year-olds who are struggling and need more support or who are bored and need more challenges. As Nutbrown (2012) identified, 2 is a key age for ensuring that children do not get left behind developmentally especially in the 'Prime Areas' she identified. Catching up in the larger groups and lower staff/child ratios of school nursery and reception classes will be more difficult for the 3–5-year-old. At the time of writing in the UK the Department of Education (DFE 2014b) requires providers to 'supply parents and carers with a short written summary of every child's development when they are between 24 and 36 months old'. The timing and the format of the assessment are not prescribed. What is required is that the developmental age that the child appears to have reached in each of the three prime areas (Personal, Social and Emotional

Development, Physical Development and Communication and Language) is described (DFE 2014a). Where there are concerns, the Development Matters grids (BAECE 2012) may act as a guide for practitioners and parents on what might be expected of children in their third year.

However, the Development Matters grids can be completely misunderstood and misused, particularly if observation and assessment are only used to identify where children are not meeting the specified early learning goals. This approach would emphasize a normative view of children's development and learning. Moss and Petrie (2002) suggest that where an outcomes or milestones perspective is taken on assessment such as this, it reveals a view of the child as 'the developmental child' who needs to be filled with knowledge in order to progress to a predetermined goal. When this happens, assessments of young children often rely on a task-based approach, whereby the child is presented with certain materials and encouraged to do certain activities. Test situations such as this do not fit well with the typical characteristics of 2-year-olds who will often be fearful or unco-operative, resulting in decontextualized, biased, unrepresentative and invalid results.

Unfortunately, this approach is still adopted in some early years settings, where nursery provision is thought to be about driving children on to meet successive goals and practitioners are being expected to use the content of the Development Matters 'Unique Child' columns to complete tick boxes. To try to avoid this approach, one North London early years advisor counsels practitioners to read the columns in 'Development Matters' (BAECE 2012) from right to left. This draws the practitioner into evaluating practice rather than making value judgements about the child.

To gather a more reliable, holistic picture of a child's development and learning, practitioners need to adopt an approach that recognizes each child's individual way of accomplishing things. Instead of looking for narrowly defined skills such as accurately pointing to a named object or drawing a vertical line, the assessment process should record the variety of ways the child demonstrates all they know and can do in the context of their everyday experiences. This is called 'Functional assessment' (Dichtelmiller and Ensler 2004) or 'formative assessment', wherein all aspects of the child's development are recorded and the way in which they interlink is made clear, as in the example below.

Case study

This is an excerpt from an assessment Andrea's Key Person made based on a collection of observations:

Andrea's (2y4m) physical strength and dexterity, spatial awareness (for example when manoeuvring the doll's buggy) and creativity (as she adopts different roles) are all working together to enable her to enjoy rich pretend play. Through this play Andrea's problem-solving skills are evident (e.g. she tries different techniques to keep her 'baby safe and buggy on track'). Her growing dispositions of determination and perseverance (Katz 1988) and her ability to maintain a high level of 'involvement' (Laevers 1994) are all helping her achieve. I have noticed how often her play includes transporting dolls, 'shopping' and other materials around the setting. This might indicate a 'transporting schema' (Athey 2003). I will continue to observe Andrea to see if this is a current interest and will introduce . . .

This approach is more appropriate for all children but particularly 2-year-olds because they are strongly affected by contextual factors such as their cultural background, current physical and emotional state and their relationship with the practitioner in how they approach activities and they do not have sufficient language to explain their difficulties in a task or test situation.

All these issues demand that settings develop a shared vision and clear principles in relation to what they assess and how they do it. A clear pedagogical ethos in this respect enables practitioners to be confident and effective in their assessment method and to be clear with parents and other professionals about why they do what they do. Confidence in their professional role allows practitioners to listen to others' views and be flexible in their approach. It is to be hoped that part of this ethos would be the principle that all planning of provision for 2-year-olds is firmly based on effective observation and assessment methods.

Planning possible routes

At worst, planning is solely an exercise in filling in a matrix with learning areas or similar in one column and days of the week across the top: a chore carried out by practitioners in turn, a room leader or the manager of a setting. This type of planning does not embrace the principles of the Unique Child (DFE 2014a) or the characteristics common to 2-year-olds. Neither does it recognize the value of all three levels of planning: long, medium and short term.

Effective long-term planning reflects the shared vision and principles that have been developed in the setting. These will be based on the practitioners' personal and professional values. For example, where closeness and warmth of relationships are valued, a setting might focus on creating cosy areas with seating and cushions for practitioners and children to sit together, relaxed meal times with practitioners and children eating together and prolonged settling-in periods. Those keen to enable young children to express themselves creatively will have permanent workshop-style mark making and construction areas. They will have abundant pretend play resources and prioritize well-planned opportunities for music and dance, for example (Manning-Morton and Thorp 2003).

Long-term plans will relate to, but not exclusively or unthinkingly follow, any local authority or statutory government guidance. Developing an explicit shared vision on which to base practice minimizes conflict between practitioners as it makes decisions less about an individual's approach and more about theoretically supported practice and agreed values and principles. This makes it more possible to make a stand against the influences of ill thought-out government policy or any unhelpful inspection requirement. This, in turn, empowers practitioners and enables them to be proud of what they provide, able to respond to individual children's circumstances rather than react solely to external forces.

The medium-term programme is about planning for the coming term or half term. It involves looking ahead at predictable events and asking how related experiences can be integrated into the provision in a way that is meaningful for 2-year-olds. Planning for the medium term provides an opportunity to review the areas of the setting indoors and out and to adapt routines according to the needs and interests of the current group of children. Events might include seasonal changes, a new child starting from a particular language group, children in transition, festivals families will be celebrating or community events (see suggested formats in Manning-Morton and Thorp 2006).

Although long- and medium-term planning are important to ensure that practitioners consider the whole context of children's learning and development, for 2-year-olds, who are in the 'here and now', it is how play opportunities are experienced every day that is meaningful. This means adopting an approach to planning in the short term that allows the curriculum to emerge from the child's current fascinations and unfold through time; this is called an 'emergent' curriculum (Edwards et al. 1994: 41). In this approach the overall environment and play opportunities stay much the same day by day but are adapted according to what is observed to happen. Children's interest is maintained and their learning extended by additional resources or a different or extra feature being introduced into the environment. This approach provides necessary opportunities for 2-year-olds to repeat activities and experiences and thereby to practise and extend their skills. The majority of the children's play and learning will be based on their free choices from the selection of resources in the carefully planned environment. However, to reflect children's schemas or information gained from parents about home events, some specific play opportunities will be planned.

High quality short-term plans will reflect practitioners' understanding of each unique child and of 2-year-olds' common characteristics and will be designed so that parents' contributions are integrated into the plan.

However, as Greenman et al. (2008: 256) assert, 'The child's entire experience within the program is important; there is no clear separation between learning and caring, play and work – certainly the child doesn't fit education into a tidy time or space.' Therefore a well-planned curriculum for 2-year-olds includes not only carefully planned play experiences but also the physical and the psychological environment, the organization of daily care routines and decisions about the organizational structure of the setting such as age grouping, group size and ratios.

Planning the structure of the provision

Munton et al. (2002), in a review of international research, identified that two of the five key variables in the quality of provision are staff: child ratios and group size, and evidence from research such as Howes et al. (1992) shows that these variables have a direct impact on the ability of staff to provide sensitive, responsive care for children. Child: adult ratios vary internationally but in the UK statutory guidance requires one adult to every four 2-year-olds (DFE 2014a). Maintaining high ratios in settings is significant not only because they enable staff to provide better quality care but because they are also associated with job satisfaction and lower staff turnover, which in turn ensures greater consistency of care, a factor that is frequently associated with good quality.

How children are grouped is also an influential factor on children's and families' experience of a group setting. Greenman et al. (2008) set out a comprehensive review of the advantages and disadvantages of same-age and mixed-age grouping. They describe how narrow age bands may reflect a Piagetian theoretical perspective, in which children are seen as best catered for within a particular stage of development. This arrangement can seem advantageous to the practitioners but has disadvantages for the children. In such groups, 2-year-olds are often grouped separately so lack the benefit of learning from older, more experienced peers or being able to regress and be 'baby-like' when they need to.

Often when children are within a narrow age range, practitioners expect them all to be the same and develop practices that treat children as a group, with identical needs, rather than reflecting the uniqueness of each child. It also means that children may change group and Key Person as frequently as every six months, which is disruptive of children's relationships and fails to provide them with continuity or consistency of experience. Some settings address this issue by Key Persons moving with their key children when they change groups.

The issues above seem to indicate that mixed-age groups are more satisfactory and, indeed, they have many advantages such as siblings being able to be together and continuity of relationships with Key Persons being maintained. Research shows that children are more likely to receive appropriate care giving and activities when they have had the same Key Person for two to three years (Raikes 1993). But there is no denying that providing an appropriate curriculum for a wide age range is very challenging, so practitioners would need to ensure that they didn't aim their planning of provision at only one end of the age range.

In order to ensure that appropriate decisions about group organization are made, Lally et al. (1997) also emphasize that leaders need experience of working in groups of younger children so that they can understand directly the powerful impact that group size, composition and dynamic can have on a young child's developing sense of self.

Planning the physical environment

Notable early childhood writers and theorists emphasize the significance of the physical environment. Malagozzi (cited in Edwards et al. 1994) describes the environment as the children's third teacher, while Piaget (cited in Cohen 2002) saw children learning through their interaction with the environment. High quality environments provide opportunities for young children to explore, problem solve, create, imagine and represent. Different environments impact differently on the way children feel and their interactions with others.

Reflective exercise

Part one

Think about an environment that you enjoy or a special place. Close your eyes and imagine that you are in that place. Look around, what can you see? Is it bright and vivid or are there calm, muted colours around you? How does that make you feel? Are you on your own or with lots of others? How is that good for you? What can you remember of the smells in your special place, are there any? What can you hear? Is it a quiet place or can you hear chatter, laughter or the sounds of nature? What about texture – warmth or softness? How significant are the sensory experiences? Note the psychological impact. What feelings does this environment evoke in you (Manning-Morton and Thorp 2006)?

How does your response to this exercise compare with the main themes arising from the responses of students listed below? They valued:

- Places that are aesthetically and sensually pleasing: the sensory experiences; the colours of the decor, of nature; the feel of rain, sun, grass on skin; the sounds of music, waves on the beach, water trickling by, music, laughter; the smell of favourite food from home, of own bed
- Feelings of belonging: being together with family, friends; a sense of community, being called by name by a neighbour over the fence, meeting people they know en route to the shops; sense of self; having their stuff around them, knowing what's where
- Freedom: of movement; to dance, run; of time; to be with friends or be alone, not be bound by routines, to be still, able to escape busy-ness, experience calmness; being free to choose, autonomy.

Part two

Looking at the list of what contributes to an adult's experience of a good environment, do you think these aspects are equally important to 2-year-olds? If so, how would you assess settings that you know in terms of the sensory experience/aesthetics, the sense of belonging they create; opportunities for free movement, choice to be close to others and also to be alone and spaces to be lively and to have calm?

Do you see any of the following?

- Lots of natural light, and artificial light that can be dimmed in areas so that children can sleep in low light, for example
- Muted colours and walls that are not too busy help to create a relaxed atmosphere and draw the eye to interesting displays
- Low room dividers enclosing activity areas enable 2-year-olds to feel contained and focused in an area but still able to keep their close adults in view, should they need to
- Windows low enough for small children to see the world outside and into other parts of the setting like the kitchen or baby room so that children spending long days in a setting can feel connected to the wider community and so feel useful.

What would you add to this list?

Environments with these features are well matched to the characteristics of 2-year-olds. However, children change, as does the composition of the group, so these aspects need to be constantly evaluated so that the uniqueness of each child continues to be reflected. A useful barometer of any environment's atmosphere is for the practitioner to regularly reflect on whether they feel relaxed, irritated, at ease or uncomfortable in the setting, as this may also be the children's experience.

The psychological environment (or hidden curriculum)

As well as the physical surroundings, feelings of ease or discomfort are equally provoked by the psychological environment of a setting. This unplanned aspect of provision may be quite unconscious yet it is one that young children learn from because they drink in all that surrounds them. This 'hidden' curriculum emerges from the practitioners' and managers' personal and professional values (Brock 2009) and only becomes conscious if these are recognized and openly discussed. For example, children may inadvertently learn that the practitioners value some abilities such as succeeding in colour-matching games more than balance and climbing skills because of the time and attention given to each of them. This, of course also applies to which children get more attention and for what kind of behaviour. For example, the boys in the group may attract more attention than the girls or displays of unacceptable behaviour may take up more practitioner time than the behaviour that practitioners want to encourage. Although this attention might be negative, it can still convey a message about what or who is seen as important. A message about what is valued and acceptable is also conveyed when a practitioner appears unwilling to discuss some topics that children introduce or ask questions about. Some children may learn that their contributions are not valued or make practitioners feel uncomfortable. These topics may relate to the child's home experience or cultural background. Children may learn that things they are familiar with at home are not appreciated or even acknowledged away from home, particularly if the resources and environment do not reflect their home culture.

Conclusion

A considerable part of this chapter has focused on and endorsed an underpinning principle of the EYFS, the 'Unique Child' (DFE 2014a). The reason for this is that only by really valuing close observation of each young child can their uniqueness be appreciated, and high quality provision planned. This was the experience of Reece, his Key Person and mother through sharing his learning stories, and Hanna's carers when discussing the observations her Key Person recorded. However, unless observation is experienced as enjoyable and really useful, it becomes another chore for busy practitioners, an external pressure from management and inspection agencies, as can planning and assessment.

Planning has been identified as much more than filling in weekly grids if it is to be meaningful to parents and children and feel worth doing by practitioners. Planning includes sharing and agreeing the values of the team and how these can be reflected in practice. It means giving thought to how the natural world and community in which the setting exists are integrated with children's experiences in the setting. At its best and most rewarding for all concerned, it is about hour-by-hour, minute-by-minute responses to children's interests and concerns. It includes the fine detail of how experiences are provided matched to the particular and common characteristics of 2-year-olds.

Effective assessment (and observation and planning) are not about individual practitioners producing reams of written work largely in their own time. Rather it emerges from dialogue between the Key Person, children, parents and colleagues. Assessment is most useful if it is an ongoing process and one that, like observation, is recorded in ways that are accessible and worthwhile for those it is intended to benefit and inform. Therefore, effective assessment does not just ask 'How well is the child doing?' It also asks 'How are structural issues such as group size, age range and the physical environment impacting on that child's learning and well-being?'

Finally, following and providing well for the different journeys of each unique 2-year-old cannot be achieved through quick jottings while children are sleeping or during lunch breaks. High quality observations, planning and assessments are only achieved if practitioners are given the time, space and support to carry out such an important aspect of their work.

10 The practitioner's journey

Introduction

In a Key Times training exercise practitioners reflect on what it's like to encounter a difficulty in a country where they do not speak or understand the language. They consistently identify feelings of anxiety, frustration, fear and bewilderment, and potential behaviours such as crying, shouting or withdrawal or perhaps manically taking control. The things they need in this situation, they say, are information and reassurance from someone who knows the area, customs and language and can help them access what they need. This is part of what the Key Person does for their key children; 2-year-olds need to know that someone in particular is looking out for them, someone who knows them well and to whom they can turn whenever they need to in this strange 'country' of the early years setting. This apparently simple role of the Key Person as companion, guide and interpreter is often underestimated, misunderstood and incorrectly implemented. It is in fact a complex role and carrying it out effectively is highly skilled, as being a guide for very young children requires not only a deep level of understanding of the children but also of oneself (Manning-Morton 2006). So, this chapter will consider the role of the Key Person working with 2-year-olds and will examine the particular skills and attributes that contribute to the well-being of the children. But as the well-being of children cannot be separated from the well-being of the practitioners (Elfer 2012; Manning-Morton 2014), this chapter will also discuss the kinds of support practitioners need on their professional journey to being effective Key Persons.

> **Case study**
>
> At a staff meeting four practitioners and their manager were doing a six-week review of provision. Esther described how her small key group time was not

going so well as Phoebe and Rosie had developed a not sitting down but rolling around game. This was making her more of a 'controller' than someone supporting close relationships in and with her key group. Dan suggested going with it by having the group time on the grassy slope in the garden for a while. Agnes said the new steps to the changing table were great for all but her new key child. She thought his aversion to having his nappy changed was about lying on the changing mat. Dan, the co-Key Person, and Agnes agreed to try letting him stand at the wash basin playing while they changed him. Tola reported back from a course on behaviour and shared what she had learned about the characteristics of 2-year-olds and how they cannot help but have 'melt down' times. She suggested that they try not telling children they needed 'time out' but 'calm down time' instead. Dan said now they had so many older and very lively 2-year-olds, what about having some outdoor play instead of 'quiet play' while the other 2-year-olds slept? After much discussion, a solution was found on how to staff this.

The key characteristics of 2-year-olds and the practitioners working with them

The case study above is an example of the attention to detail, concern for individual children, flexibility and reflexive practice that are required of practitioners working with 2-year-olds. As highlighted throughout this book, 2-year-olds have particular characteristics and approaches to life and learning. This requires practitioners who work with 2-year-olds to have particular skills and characteristics of their own. The third year of life involves varied and rapid developmental changes, so practitioners need comprehensive knowledge of developmental pathways at this age and also in-depth understanding of each individual child. Practitioners who appreciate the complexity of the development of 2-year-olds will not make the mistake of seeing them as either less able over-3s who disrupt 'proper' activities or too-boisterous babies who don't need their support any more. Practitioners with this level of knowledge understand that 2-year-olds are not 'terrible', neither are they cute little things to be manipulated or tricked with gimmicks; they show respect for 2-year-olds as people.

However, it is not just rapid development that is a key characteristic of 2-year-olds; it is also their changeability, particularly emotionally and behaviourally. It is a characteristic that can be a distinct challenge for practitioners, as they need to be able to respond flexibly, but at the same time maintain as much consistency as possible for 2-year-olds to feel secure. The behaviours that can arise from 2-year-olds' fluctuating emotional states and their limited social skills and understanding mean that practitioners need to have a mature approach and feel positively challenged by 2-year-olds.

Being adaptable is also important in relation to each individual child's temperament, dispositions and personality. Personality development is a central focus for 2-year-olds; they will do what you *do*, not what you say, imitating the Key Person's way of speaking, touching and relating to others. So practitioners need to provide positive models of kind, friendly behaviour and open, interested attitudes from which 2-year-olds will learn. This social learning, like all aspects of their learning, is very rapid. Two-year-olds are constantly meeting new, challenging and sometimes overwhelming experiences but are also keen to practise their autonomy and independence. They then need the practitioner to provide a secure-base to help them balance these opposing drives. In providing a secure-base (as discussed in Chapter 8), the Key Person is maintaining a delicate balance between the need to keep children safe and the need to let them grow into confident, independent people. Because the child internalizes the practitioner's messages about when it's OK to explore and when it's not, it's useful for practitioners to reflect on how much and why they say things like 'careful' or 'get down'; are they giving the child a necessary message about a real danger? Or are they expressing their own anxieties? Equally though, practitioners must make sure that they are available when needed and that encouragements to 'off you go and play' are not rejections of a child's need for closeness. In this way effective practitioners are able to understand 2-year-olds' need for autonomy but also accept their need to retreat into dependency and physical closeness.

As we discussed in Chapter 9 with regards to planning, understanding each child's changing needs requires 'tuning in' to the meaning of 2-year-olds' behaviour and language. By listening actively and carefully and reflecting back to the child what they see happening, practitioners are supporting children's emotional literacy (Sharp 2011). However, providing such a commentary also requires that practitioners can converse naturally and not feel self-conscious when the limited language of some 2-year-olds means that there is little verbal response.

Key to the practitioner's skill is the ability to 'contain' the whole range of 2-year-olds' feeling states, from excitement to despair, as they have periods of greater or lesser fragility. By being open to, sustaining and empathetically responding to 2-year-olds' emotional needs, practitioners are supporting children's developing sense of self.

Container-contained

'Container-contained' is described by Judy Shuttleworth as the way in which a mother is able to mentally and emotionally 'hold' a child's distressed and uncomfortable feelings, which would otherwise be too much for the child to bear on their own (Shuttleworth 1989: 28). When this is a positive containing process, the adult is able to perceive the baby's state and get a feeling for what they really need and the baby experiences being 'kept in mind' and emotionally 'held'. Through anticipating and sensitively responding to her child through touch, proximity and voice tone, the mother not only 'holds' the child's anxiety but also transforms it. Bion describes this as a kind of detoxifying process that allows the baby to get back their good feelings of being held and understood (Bion 1962, cited in Bateman and Holmes 1995). This enables the child to think about and make sense of their experience and eventually to manage their anxiety more on their own.

Sustaining the impact of a child's state of mind at times of distress or anger can be disturbing and emotionally draining for the practitioner, who may then seek ways of avoiding responding to a child by quickly passing them to someone else, or by telling them they are 'making a fuss', for example. This avoidance often arises because caring for young children and experiencing an intense engagement with their feelings can stir up unconscious memories. This can put practitioners in touch with their own baby-like feelings, which may not be pleasant or welcome, particularly when the feelings are of distress or discomfort, although there are practitioners who also find children's expressions of joy or excitement hard to cope with too. Therefore a key competence of practitioners working with 2-year-olds is well-developed intrapersonal skills. This element of emotional intelligence (Goleman 1996) involves 'the capacity to understand oneself, to have an effective working model of oneself – including one's own desires, fears and capacities – and to use such information effectively in regulating one's own life' (Gardner 1999: 43).

Case study

Finn is Key Person to both Jake (2y5m) and Eddy (2y5m). Jake is enthusiastic about everything whereas Eddy is extremely cautious. Recent nearby building work fascinated Jake who loudly imitated the pneumatic drill in his pretend play. In contrast, Eddy decided he did not want to play outdoors throughout this time and was very anxious about the noise.

In their weekly planning and review meeting, Jo, their manager, began as usual by asking Finn and his co-worker, Kelly, about their key children. She noticed some uncertainty in Finn's voice as he talked about Eddy's reluctance to go outside, so asked him what he was thinking and feeling about the situation. Finn remarked that he didn't understand why Eddy was afraid, as 'he can see it's only a drill making the noise'. When Jo asked him to reflect on this comment in relation to what he knows about 2-year-olds' development, Finn could immediately see that his expectation of Eddy to be able to both understand and tolerate the intrusiveness of the drill noise was unreasonable. Kelly added that she empathized with Eddy's response because she had always been afraid of passing building sites as a child and she remembered her mum carrying her past them, which was why she found Jake's enthusiasm slightly irritating! Finn laughed and replied that his mum would have made him walk past whether he was scared or not! At this point Jo suggested that both practitioners use their journals later to reflect on how their own early experiences were impacting on their responses to both Eddy and Jake in this regard. They then moved on to discuss how to plan for both children's needs and interests, given what they had observed.

At their next meeting Finn reported that their discussion and using his journal to reflect on his ideas about boys being afraid had helped him to understand both children better and to avoid giving Eddy negative messages about his responses.

Why be an early years practitioner?

The special skills required of practitioners working with our youngest children have long been recognized by people such as Elinor Goldschmied (Goldschmied and Jackson 2004) and Anne Stonehouse (1988). But, as the case study above illustrates, in addition to these skills practitioners also need to be enthusiastic and motivated about their work, reflective of their practice and have emotional conviction as well as intellectual knowledge about good practice (Manning-Morton and Thorp 2003).

An essential part of this kind of professionalism is the ability to reflect on our personal histories and motivations (Manning-Morton 2006, 2011; Elfer 2012). In order to better understand children, we not only have to know about all aspects of their development, learning and socio-cultural contexts, we have to know ourselves: what our motivations and personal values are and how these impact on our practice.

When asked what they enjoy about work with young children, practitioners on Key Times courses identify the following:

- Seeing the children develop and flourish
- Seeing children engrossed in their play

- Seeing a child's excitement, enthusiasm and joy
- Building warm relationships with children, parents and colleagues
- The children running to greet you when you enter the room, shouting your name and hugging you, no other job has this experience
- Giving a child the cuddle they need and making them feel better.

These comments reveal that working with young children can be immensely satisfying, personally as well as professionally, and they reflect the image that most early childhood practitioners have of themselves (along with others in the helping professions), that is, to help others and to make a better world for children. However, the danger here is that the personal gratification in these positive interactions may also be filling a personal need in the practitioner. In their study of a day care setting in the late 1970s, Bain and Barnett (1986) identified that the early personal experiences of some practitioners, such as unresolved issues of early separation or lack of love and attention, influenced their choice of career as a possible means to fulfil previously unmet needs. This can clearly be a drawback because, as students are quick to identify, the practitioner who, for example, picks a child up for a cuddle when the child is happily involved in play, is not considering the child's needs. In addition, it will often be the case that practitioners' own needs will not be met at work, because the positive list above is only one half of the picture. As we can see from the list below, practitioners also identify many difficulties in their work, which, if not addressed, may then result in them feeling angry and resentful towards children, parents, managers or co-workers.

- Being overloaded with unrealistic expectations
- Constant complaining
- When there is dirt and loads of mess
- When the room is really noisy and busy
- Stress
- Conflict and bad communication
- Being bogged down with paperwork.

The problem here is not that practitioners have these needs and feelings but that they may not be aware of them. When a practitioner can understand that their difficulty with a particular child or situation is influenced by their own early experience, they are then more able to step back and understand what is going on and thereby temper their responses, as Finn in the case study was able to do. But where such feelings are denied and repressed in practitioners, they can lead to denying and repressing children's feelings and needs too. This may happen because the feelings are too uncomfortable for the practitioner or because the culture of the setting considers having these emotions to be a professional weakness (Manning-Morton 2011). What is needed instead is a setting ethos that understands that professional practice with 2-year-olds is essentially emotional and relational and that to be responsive to the social and emotional well-being of very young children requires practitioners to combine personal responsiveness and closeness with a professional perspective within the Key Person Approach (Manning-Morton 2006; Elfer et al. 2011; Elfer 2012).

What it means to be a Key Person

When reflecting on what young children value about their Key Person, practitioners consistently identify that as 2-year-olds they want a Key Person who:

- Loves me and cuddles me when I'm scared or upset
- Plays with me, reads me stories and sings me songs
- Listens to me and talks to me
- Knows what I like and what I need; feeds me and changes my nappy
- Likes me, smiles at me and makes me laugh
- Likes my mummy.

It is useful to note what is present and absent from this list and how it might differ from a practitioner's list. For example, practitioners might have included writing assessment records or activity plans as important aspects of the Key Person's role, aspects that are notably absent from what is important from a young child's perspective! For them it is the concrete relational experience of their Key Person being physically and emotionally available, responsive and closely involved in their play, as well as taking primary responsibility for their physical care that is meaningful.

What is more, children understand their relationship with their Key Person through 'reading' the practitioner's facial expressions, gestures, degree of eye contact and tone of voice and how close or far away from them they are. In turn, by engaging in attuned interactions, the practitioner connects with the child's mind and mirrors back to them who they are. Siegel (1999) suggests that in secure attachment relationships this is the fundamental way in which children develop psychological resilience and emotional well-being.

Reflective exercise

Spend some time reflecting on your non-verbal interactions, or if you are brave, pair up with a colleague and spend time observing each other's body language.

- Are you giving signals that you don't mean to?
- What are your facial expressions and tone of voice conveying to children, parents and colleagues?
- Is there anything that you could usefully change?
- Identify one example of a time when you have engaged in an attuned interaction with each of your key children. Is this easier to identify with some children than others? Why might this be?

Remember, if doing this in pairs, be kind and respectful to each other!

Attunement

Stern describes 'affect attunement' (1998) as the process whereby an adult sensitively reads a child's non-verbal signals and is then able to align their state of mind with the child to engage with them in the way they need, mirroring the child's inner state with their behaviours and vocalizations (Stern 1985). The child experiences this as 'feeling felt' and 'being understood'. Attunement then is the way in which infants and young children come to understand that their internal feeling states are shared and understood by others. Stern outlines that this happens through the adult performing actions that correspond with the child's overt behaviours (Stern 1998). In *Diary of a Baby* (1990) he illustrates this by describing how a mother's vocal response of 'YeaaAAaah!' precisely mirrored the length of time of her child's facial expressions, thereby also intuitively reflecting the rise and fall of his inner feeling with her vocal pitch.

As adults we value the people we are close to in our lives because they understand us well, accept our good and bad sides and give us their time and attention when we need it. These people are 'there for us', they trust and love us and we them; there is reciprocity, give and take. These relationships are usually long-standing and have shared experiences, with fun and humour often being key ingredients. In these relationships we feel confident and worthwhile; we can be 'ourselves'. When children feel like this, they are more likely to be able to engage in complex and creative play, freely access a broad curriculum and take risks in their learning through guessing, experimenting and making mistakes. So 2-year-olds also need these kinds of relationships with familiar and trusted adults that will enable them to develop healthy emotional attachments and a positive sense of self. By adopting a Key Person approach that emphasizes the centrality of warm, loving and secure relationships to their practice (BAECE 2012), practitioners will be supporting children to feel good about themselves and be confident.

However, as identified above, sustaining the high level of intense emotional and behavioural changes that working with 2-year-olds entails, means that practitioners may seek to defend themselves psychologically by avoiding or denying the need for such relationships. Research has shown how practitioners frequently avoid close, consistent interactions with children (Smith and Vernon 1994; Goldschmied and Jackson 2004; Manning-Morton 2006; Elfer et al. 2011) despite being aware of the importance of children receiving emotionally close and consistent attention. This defensiveness and avoidance are often manifested through raising objections or difficulties with the Key Person approach such as, 'it takes away from the parent', 'children get too close to you then get upset when you're not there', 'children need to get used to everyone'. Elfer et al. (2003: 7–9) summarize the most common objections to implementing the Key Person Approach and set out explanations and counter-arguments for each.

Further to this, practitioners may deny children's needs in other aspects of practice too. Caring for many children at once can mean practitioners welcome children who do not make demands on them, so they may think precocious self-reliance is positive and encourage independence in ways for which a child is not ready. It may be thought that requiring young children to do things for themselves such as play alone ensures that they develop resilience, yet children can only feel confident in what they can do on their own if they are given sensitive support in the first instance. As Goldschmied and Jackson write:

> Real sociability comes through the experience of the reliable affection of a few close people. Human beings have great resilience and some individuals show an amazing capacity to catch up and recover from damaging early experiences, but many do not. There is no excuse for us to repeat the ignorant mistakes of the past in the care we provide for young children today.
>
> (2004: 41)

Goldschmied and Elfer's work, along with the Key Person approach being made a practice requirement in the Early Years Foundation Stage Framework (DCSF 2008a), has encouraged huge strides to be made in improving the implementation of the Key Person Approach in group settings. However, unless the underlying issues for individual practitioners are explored and the unspoken rivalries and jealousies that arise between practitioners and with parents are acknowledged and addressed, the denial of close personal relationships will continue to be a serious flaw in most group day care (Goldschmied and Jackson 2004).

Supporting the practitioner's journey

It is clear from the issues discussed above that the positive contribution of early years provision to the social and emotional well-being of children is critically dependent on the social and emotional well-being of early years practitioners. In order to effectively meet the needs of 2-year-olds, practitioners need to develop close Key Person relationships with children and to communicate well with parents and other practitioners. This demands high levels of interpersonal and intrapersonal skills on the part of the practitioner but, as Elfer (1996), Stonehouse (1988) and Manning-Morton (2006) emphasize, to develop these skills, practitioners need opportunities in the workplace for supportive, reflective supervision from skilled, knowledgeable managers. This process should be a dialogue within which reflective practice takes place.

Reflective practice is a process through which changes in professional work are brought about in order to improve the experiences offered to the children. Moon (2005) suggests that reflective practice is about learning through and from experience; this means not only being self-aware but also challenging assumptions about everyday practice. In the case study the practitioners use a journal to aid their reflective thinking but other methods may be preferred by individuals according to their learning style. Bolton (2005) suggests that discussion with colleagues about significant incidents, or simply pausing and thinking through the day or the week, are also valuable. Reflecting in this way may not always offer a solution but can help to clarify one's thinking about a situation and thereby lead to a change in perspective or to a different course of action next time.

The Tickell Review (2011) suggests that 'supervision should be expressed in such a way that encourages reflective practice and moves away from the perception that it is merely a tick-box approach to check what practitioners are, or are not, doing' (Tickell 2011: 5.17). This is useful because although the *Statutory Framework for the Early Years Foundation Stage* states that: 'Providers must put appropriate arrangements in place for the supervision of staff who have contact with children and families' (DFE 2014a: 3.21), it is clear from discussions with students and practitioners that the term 'supervision' means different things to different people. Supervision in settings is often combined with appraisal so often does not create the kind of trusting atmosphere in which both personal and professional self-development issues are addressed (Whalley 2001).

It is the responsibility of those who are in a leadership and management position to provide regular support and supervision sessions and opportunities for professional reflection through creating a working culture and suitable times and spaces for practitioners to pause and reflect on their work experiences. In two recent projects, one focussed on well-being (Manning-Morton 2014) and one on 2-year-olds (Liverpool City Council, Quality Improvement team (EYFS)), a key issue identified by practitioners as being essential to but missing from their practice was time: time to just be with the children, time to observe and time to reflect and discuss.

Being a leader of provision for 2-year-olds

In this context, leaders and managers of provision for 2-year-olds not only need knowledge and experience of the complex and demanding nature of the work but also highly developed communication skills. Elfer and Dearnley (2007) also discuss the importance of leaders and managers deepening their understanding of the dynamics of groups so that leaders may better support practitioners in developing positive relationships with children.

So, in the same way as practitioners support children's emotional well-being and development in the knowledge that they are supporting their all-round learning, managers and trainers must pay attention to the emotional as well as theoretical learning of practitioners in their supervision and training opportunities (Manning-Morton 2006). As Peter Elfer says, 'It is difficult to sustain close and responsive relationships with young children without an organisational culture that expects and supports a process of reflection on the emotional dimension of practice' (1996: 30).

This focus on the relational aspects of leadership is also the approach taken in Zero to Three's Leadership Development Initiative in the USA (Kellegrew and Youcha 2004). This model emphasizes that 'knowing' (about children from different perspectives) and 'doing' (taking action to influence positive outcomes for children and families) are equally important abilities for leaders but that change is embedded in the context of social relationships, both personal and professional.

Reflective exercise

If you are a leader of provision for 2-year-olds, reflect on the areas of knowledge and skill that you think you need to develop further.

- Where and how might you go about obtaining this? Who do you get support from?
- If you are a practitioner, reflect on the supervision and training you receive. Does it help you to consider the emotional aspects of your practice?
- Make a wish list of the kinds of support you need to further develop your practice.

It is clear then that in order to facilitate useful supervision discussions, leaders and managers need to develop their own interpersonal skills. This includes asking open-ended questions and engaging in active listening to voice tone and body language as well as words such as illustrated by Jo in the case study: hearing exactly what the practitioner has said – not what you think they have said (Whitaker 1995).

Leaders of settings also need to be able to maintain perspective when working with social disadvantage, challenging behaviours, intimate family issues and family or staff distress. This often means providing the same kind of 'containment' function for practitioners and families as parents and practitioners do for children. However, like practitioners need to do with 2-year-olds' dependence and independence, leaders and managers also need to balance the need to support practitioners with the need to allow them to act as capable adults. Some managers deny the needs of their teams, busying themselves with paperwork in the office. Others seem to thrive on being needed, so collude with team members when they behave dependently, by solving all their problems for them and taking on tasks which are not theirs. This 'rescuing' behaviour (Steiner 1974) not only infantilizes another adult, it also cannot be sustained, often resulting in burn-out (and subsequent absence) of the manager or resentful blaming of practitioners when things get too much.

Therefore, leaders and managers also need to develop self-awareness in order to understand when they might be perpetuating their own patterns of behaviour or reacting from a place that is more to do with their own early experiences rather than the reality of the current situation. This kind of self-awareness can be developed by keeping a reflective journal (Bolton 2005) in which common themes may be identified over time. It can also help just to slow down and think about your emotional reaction before responding to someone or something, temporarily holding all the feelings and issues that have been presented to you. Keeping a journal helps the thinking process about why something happened, how you felt about it, what you think the practitioner/family/team want from you and how you want to respond. Leaders who were part of the Emotional Well-being: Strong Teams training in a London borough identified that keeping a journal 'helps me get a perspective so I no longer take work home with me in my head so much. I also have more focus so things are dealt with; journaling helps with this.' These leaders also identified that being part of a reflective supervision group enabled them to be more available to their teams on one hand but to also stand back and allow more autonomy on the other (Manning-Morton and Wilson 2011).

Professional self-esteem

It is to be hoped that, through facilitating high levels of reflection and professional self-development, managers and leaders would be engendering professional competence and confidence in themselves and their team members. Such professional confidence is still often lacking in practitioners working with babies, toddlers and 2-year-olds, who, unlike their colleagues working with older children, seem not yet to have reaped the benefit of higher regard in the field. Working with the youngest children is still less valued as it has connotations of being somehow less skilled intellectually. It is our contention of course that there is nothing further from the truth, yet still examples of management practice that reinforce this view persist, for example, the deployment of practitioners with Early Years Professional Status or Early Years Teacher Status being more likely with older children or sending less experienced staff on courses that are for managers in relation to 2-year-olds rather than attending themselves. These kinds of messages about how work with this age group is valued are received by practitioners as a lack of external validation, which can lead to a negative sense of professional worth, which impacts negatively on practice.

Lally et al. (1997) suggest that providing well for our youngest children requires leaders to have both a solid grounding in early development and learning and experience of working with groups of young children. They go on to say that often leaders have one of these attributes but seldom have both, a situation that they suggest leads to inappropriate organizational decision making for 0–3s provision, such as group sizes that are too large or staffing arrangements that do not support attachment relationships (Lally et al. 1997). Manning-Morton (2004), in reference to UK policy, raises the concern that managers of new children's centres are more and more frequently headteachers of schools with none of the grounding in the care and education of 0–3-year-olds that Lally et al. suggest is crucial, a situation that is increasing due to the expansion of provision in schools for 2-year-olds.

Conclusion

Working with 2-year-olds is a joy and a challenge and requires highly developed knowledge and understanding of the children and of oneself. In order to effectively carry out the demanding and skilful role of a Key Person working with 2-year-olds, practitioners need their joys and successes affirmed and celebrated and their dilemmas and difficulties listened to and addressed. In turn, this requires that leaders and managers have highly developed communication skills and that they provide regular opportunities for reflective supervision in which all aspects of the work can be discussed. Above all, practitioners, leaders and managers should value this area of work for the importance it carries in relation to very young children's lives.

References

Abbott, L. and Langston, A. (eds) (2005) *Birth to Three Matters: Supporting the Framework of Effective Practice*. Maidenhead: OUP McGraw-Hill Education.

Ahadi, S.A. and Robarth, M.K. (1994) Temperament development and the Big Five, in C.F. Halvorsen, G.A. Kohnstamm, and R.P. Martin (eds) *The Developing Structure of Temperament and Personality from Infancy to Adulthood*. Hillsdale, NJ: Erlbaum.

Ainsworth, M., Blehar, M., Waters, E. and Wall, S. (1978) *Patterns of Attachment: Assessed in the Strange Situation and at Home*. New Jersey: Erlbaum.

Ames, L.B. and Ilg, F.L. (1976) *Your Two Year Old: Terrible or Tender?* New York: Dell Publishing.

Athey, C. (2003) *Extending Thought in Young Children*. London: Paul Chapman.

BAECE (2012) *Development Matters in the Early Years Foundation Stage (EYFS)*. Available at: http://www.foundationyears.org.uk/files/2012/03/Development-Matters-FINAL-PRINT-AMENDED.pdf (accessed 08/08/2014).

Bain, A. and Barnett, L. (1986) *The Design of a Day Care System in a Nursery Setting for Children Under Five*. London: Tavistock Institute of Human Relations

Barker, E., Copeland, W., Maughn, B., Jaffee, S. and Uher, R. (2012) Relative impact of maternal depression and associated risk factors on offspring psychopathology. *British Journal of Psychiatry*, February (200): 124–9.

Barlow, J., Coren, E. and Stewart-Brown, S. (2002) Meta-analysis of the effectiveness of parenting programmes in improving maternal psychosocial health. *British Journal of General Practice*, 52(476): 223–33.

Barnes. J., Leach P., Sylva, P., Stein A., Malmberg, L. and the FCCC team (2006) Infant care in England: Mothers' aspirations, experiences, satisfaction and caregiver relationships. *Early Child Development and Care*, 176(5): 553–73.

Bateman, A. and Holmes, J. (1995) *An Introduction to Psychoanalysis: Contemporary Theory and Practice*. London: Routledge.

Baumrind, D. (1966) Effects of authoritative parental control on child behaviour. *Child Development* 37(4): 887–907.

Baumrind, D. (1991) The influence of parenting style on adolescent competence and substance use, *Journal of Early Adolescence*, 11(1): 56–95.

Bee, H. (2000) *The Developing Child*, 9th edn. Boston, MA: Allyn and Bacon.

Berk, L.E. (2009) *Child Development*, 8th edn. Boston: Pearson.

Berk, L.E. (2012) *Child Development*. Boston: Pearson.

Berne, E. (1970) *Transactional Analysis in Psychotherapy*. New York: Ballantine Books.

Blakemore, C. (1998) *The Mind Machine*. London: BBC Books.

Bloom, K. (2006) *The Embodied Self: Movement and Psychoanalysis*. London: Karnac Books.

Bolton, G. (2005) *Reflective Practice: Writing and Professional Development*. London: Sage Publications.

Bowlby, J. (1973) *Attachment and Loss Vol. 2: Separation*. Harmondsworth: Penguin.

Bowlby, J. (1988) *A Secure Base: Clinical Applications of Attachment Theory*. London: Routledge.

Bowlby, J. (2005) *The Making and Breaking of Affectional Bonds*. London: Routledge.

Brice-Heath, S. (1983) *Ways with Words: Language, Life and Work in Communities and Classrooms*. Cambridge: Cambridge University Press.

Brock, J. (2009) Curriculum and pedagogy of play: a multitude of perspectives, in J. Brock, S. Dodds, P. Jarvis and Y. Olusoga *Perspectives on Play: Learning for Life*. Harlow: Pearson Education.

Bronfenbrenner, U. (1979) *The Ecology of Human Development: Experiments by Nature and Design*. Cambridge, MA: Harvard University Press.

Brook, P.J. and Kempe, V. (2014) *Encyclopaedia of Language Development*. London: Sage Publications.

Brooker, L. (2010) Constructing the triangle of care: power and professionalism in practitioner/parent relationships. *British Journal of Educational Studies*, 58(2): 181–96.

Brown, B. (2001) *Combating Discrimination: Persona Dolls in Action*. London: Trentham Books.

Bruce, T. (2001) *Learning through Play: Babies, Toddlers and the Foundation Years*. London: Hodder and Stoughton.

Bruce, T. (2011) *Early Childhood Education*. London: Hodder Education.

Bruer, J. (1997) Education and the brain: a bridge too far. *Educational Researcher*, 26(8): 4–16.

Bruner, J.S. (1977) Early social interaction and language acquisition, in H.R. Schaffer (ed.) *Studies of Mother-Infant Interaction*. London: Academic Press.

Burningham, J. (2000) *Harvey Slumpfenberger's Christmas Present*. London: Walker Books.

Buss, A. and Plomin, R. (1984) *Temperament: Early Developing Personality Traits.* Hillsdale, NJ: Lawrence Erlbaum Associates Inc.

Buss, A. and Plomin, R. (1986) The EAS approach to temperament, in R. Plomin and J. Dunn (eds) *The Study of Temperament: Changes, Continuities and Challenges.* Hillsdale, NJ: Lawrence Erlbaum Associates Inc.

Carr, M. and Lee, W. (2012) *Learning Stories: Constructing Learner Identities in Early Education.* London: Sage Publications.

Carroll, R. (2001) *The Autonomic Nervous System: Barometer of Intensity and Internal Conflict.* Available at: http://www.thinkbody.co.uk/papers/autonomic-nervous-system.htm (accessed 25/06/2014).

Carroll, R. (2004) Emotion and embodiment: A new relationship between neuroscience and psychotherapy. Training manual, unpublished.

Carter, R. (1998) *Mapping the Mind.* London: Seven Dials.

Cheal, D. (2002) *Sociology of Family Life.* Basingstoke: Palgrave.

Children's Food Trust (2012) *Eat Better, Start Better: Voluntary Food and Drink Guidelines for Early Years Settings in England – A Practical Guide.* Available at: http://www.childrensfoodtrust.org.uk/assets/eat-better-start-better/CFT%20Early%20Years%20Guide_Interactive_Sept%2012.pdf (accessed 30/07/2012).

Clark, A. (2009) *Listening as a Way of Life.* The Young Children's Voices Network, National Children's Bureau. Available at: http://www.ncb.org.uk/media/74018/an_introduction_to_why_and_how_we_listen_to_very_young_children.pdf (accessed 31/07/2014).

Clark, A. (2010) *Transforming Children's Spaces: Children's and Adults' Participation in Designing Learning Environments.* London: Routledge.

Clark, R.M. (2010) *Childhood in Society for Early Childhood Studies.* Exeter: Learning Matters.

Clarke, P. (1992) *English as a 2nd Language in Early Childhood.* Victoria, Australia: Free Kindergarten Association, Multicultural Resource Centre.

Cohen, D. (2002) *How the Child's Mind Develops.* Hove: Routledge.

Crain, W. (1992) *Theories of Development: Concepts and Applications.* New Jersey: Prentice-Hall.

Dalli, C. and Kibble, N. (2010) Peaceful caregiving as curriculum: Insights on primary caregiving from action research. In A. Meade (ed.) *Dispersing Waves: Innovation in Early Childhood Education.* New Zealand: NZCER Press.

Davies, M. (2003) *Movement and Dance in Early Childhood,* 2nd edn. London: Sage.

DCSF (Department for Children, Schools and Families) (2008a) *The Early Years Foundation Stage: Setting the Standards for Learning,*

Development and Care for Children from Birth to Five. London: DCSF.

DCSF (Department for Children, Schools and Families (2008b) *Every Child a Talker: Guidance for Early Language Lead Practitioners.* Available at: http://webarchive.nationalarchives.gov.uk/20130401151715/https:/www.education.gov.uk/publications/eOrderingDownload/DCSF-00854-2008.pdf (accessed 08/08/2014).

DCSF (Department for Children, Schools and Families) (2008c) *The Early Years Foundation Stage: Principles into Practice Card No. 2.4.* Nottingham: DCSF Publications.

Derman-Sparks, L. and Olsen Edwards, J. (2010) *Anti-bias Education for Young Children and Ourselves.* Washington, DC: NAEYC.

DFE (Department for Education) (2011) *Rolling out Free Early Education for Disadvantaged Two Year Olds: An Implementation Study for Local Authorities and Providers.* National Children's Bureau with National Centre for Social Research. Available at: http://www.natcen.ac.uk/media/26401/rolling-out-free-early-education.pdf (accessed 08/08/2014).

DFE (Department for Education) (2013a) *Press Release: £755 Million to Double Free Childcare Offer for 2-Year-Olds.* Available at: https://www.gov.uk/government/news/755-million-to-double-free-childcare-offer-for-2-year-olds (accessed 24/08/2014).

DFE (Department for Education) (2013b) *Research and Analysis: The Early Education Pilot for 2-Year-Old Children: Age 5 Follow Up. Follow-up Evaluation of the Early Education Pilot for 2-year-old Children.* Available at: https://www.gov.uk/government/publications/the-early-education-pilot-for-two-year-old-children-age-five-follow-up (accessed 24/08/2014).

DFE (Department for Education) (2014a) *Statutory Framework for the Early Years Foundation Stage. Setting the Standards for Learning, Development and Care for Children from Birth to Five.* Available at: https://www.gov.uk/government/uploads/system/uploads/attachment_data/file/335504/EYFS_framework_from_1_September_2014__with_clarification_note.pdf (accessed 04/08/2014).

DFE (Department for Education) (2014b) *Guidance: Progress Check at Age 2 and EYFS Profile.* Available at: https://www.gov.uk/progress-check-at-age-2-and-eyfs-profile (accessed 08/08/2014).

DfES (Department for Education and Schools), Sure Start (2002) *Birth to Three Matters: A Framework to Support Children in their Earliest Years.* London: DfES.

Dichtelmiller, M.L. and Ensler, L. (2004) Infant toddler assessment: one program's experience. *Young Children,* January 2004: 30–3.

Dickins, M. (2014) Young children's well-being in times of austerity, in J. Manning-Morton (ed.) *Exploring Well-being in the Early Years.* Maidenhead: Open University Press/McGraw-Hill Education.

Donaldson, J. (1999) *The Gruffalo*. London: Macmillan Children's Books.

Dowling, M. (2005) *Young Children's Personal, Social and Emotional Development*. London: Paul Chapman Publishing.

Dowling, M. (2010) *Young Children's Personal, Social and Emotional Development*. London: Paul Chapman Publishing.

Duffy, A., Chambers, F., Croughan, S. and Stephens, J. (2006) *Working with Babies and Toddlers*. Oxford: Heinemann.

Dunn, J. (1988) *The Beginnings of Social Understanding*. Oxford: Blackwell.

Dunn, J. (2004) *Children's Friendships: The Beginnings of Intimacy*. Oxford: Blackwell Publishing.

Dunn, J., Brown, J., Slomkowski, C., Tesla, C. and Youngblade, L.M. (1991) Young children's understanding of other people's feelings and beliefs: individual differences and their antecedents. *Child Development*, 62: 1352–66.

Dweck, C.S. (2000) *Self-theories: Their Role in Motivation, Personality, and Development*. Philadelphia: Psychology Press.

Education Scotland (2010) *Pre-birth to Three: Positive Outcomes for Scotland's Children and Families*. Available at: http://www.educationscotland.gov.uk/thecurriculum/whatiscurriculumforexcellence/learningthroughoutlife/prebirthto3.asp (accessed 10/08/2014).

Edwards, C. Gandini, L. and Forman, G. (1994) *The Hundred Languages of Children: The Reggio Emilia Approach to Early Childhood Education*. Norwood, NJ: Ablex Publishing.

Elfer, P. (1996) Building intimacy in relationships with young children in nurseries. *Early Years*, 16(2): 30–4.

Elfer, P. (2005) Observation matters, in L. Abbott and A. Langston (eds) *Birth to Three Matters: Supporting the Framework of Effective Practice*. Maidenhead: Open University Press/McGraw-Hill Education.

Elfer, P. (2012) Emotion in nursery work: work discussion as a model of critical professional reflection. *Early Years Journal of International Research and Development*, 32(2): 129–41.

Elfer, P. and Dearnley, K. (2007) Nurseries and emotional well being: evaluating an emotionally containing model of professional development. *Early Years: An International Journal of Research and Development*, 27(3): 267–79.

Elfer, P., Goldschmied, E. and Selleck, D.Y. (2011) *Key Persons in the Early Years: Building Relationships for Quality Provision in Early Years Settings and Primary Schools*. London: Routledge.

Eliot, L. (1999) *Early Intelligence: How the Brain and Mind Develop in the First Five Years of Life*. London: Penguin.

Erikson, E. (1967) *Childhood and Society*, 2nd edn. London: Penguin.

Family Lives (2014) Parents value advice & support from organisations according to new survey on family life. Available at: http://www.

familylives.org.uk/about/press/parents-value-advice-support-from-organisations-according-to-new-survey-on-family-life/ (accessed 24/08/2014).

Fawcett, M. (2009) *Learning Through Child Observation*. London: Jessica Kingsley Publishers.

Fitzgerald, D. (2004) *Parent Partnership in the Early Years*. London: Continuum.

Fraleigh, S.H. (1999) *Dancing into Darkness: Butoh, Zen, and Japan*. Pittsburgh, PA: University of Pittsburgh Press.

Gandini, L. (1998) Educational and caring spaces, in C. Edwards, L. Gandini and G. Forman (eds) *The Hundred Languages of Children: The Reggio Emilia Approach to Early Childhood Education – Advanced Reflections*. Norwood, NJ: Ablex.

Garcia, F. and Garcia, E. (2009) Is authoritative always the optimum parenting style? Evidence from Spanish families. *Adolescence*, 44(173): 101–31.

Gardner, H. (1999) *Intelligence Reframed: Multiple Intelligences for the 21st Century*. New York: Basic Books.

Gerber, M. (2005) RIE practices and principles, in S. Petrie and S. Owen *Authentic Relationships in Group Care for Infants and Toddlers – Resources for Infant Educarers* (RIE) *Principles into Practice*. London: Jessica Kingsley Publishers.

Gerhardt, S. (2004) *Why Love Matters: How Affection Shapes a Baby's Brain*. Hove: Brunner-Routledge.

Goddard-Blythe, S. (2004) *The Well Balanced Child: Movement and Early Learning*. Stroud: Hawthorne Press.

Goldschmied, E. and Jackson, S. (2004) *People Under Three: Young Children in Day Care*. London: Routledge.

Goldschmied, E. and Selleck, D. (1996) *Communication between Babies in their First Year*. London: National Children's Bureau. (Video and booklet)

Goleman, D. (1996) *Emotional Intelligence: Why It Can Matter More than IQ*. London: Bloomsbury Publishing.

Golombok, S. (2000) *Parenting: What Really Counts?* Hove: Routledge.

Gopnik, A., Meltzoff, A. and Kuhl, P. (1999) *How Babies Think*. London: Weidenfeld and Nicolson.

Goswami, U. (1998) *Cognition in Children*. Hove: Psychology Press.

Greenland, P. (2005) *Developmental Movement Play: Emerging Themes from a Six Year Project Exploring Physical Development Practice in the Early Yyears*. Leeds: JABADO Publications.

Greenland, P. (2009) *Developmental Movement Play: Final Report and Recommendations from a 10-Year Action Research Project Investigating the Way the Early Years Sector Supports the Youngest Children to be Fully Physical*. Available at: http://www.jabadao.org/storage/downloads/More_of_Me_Full_Report.pdf (accessed 30/06/2014).

Greenman, J. and Stonehouse, A. (1996) *Prime Times: A Handbook for Excellence in Infant Toddler Programs.* St. Paul, MN: Redleaf Press.

Greenman, J., Stonehouse, A. and Schweikert, G. (2008) *Prime Times: A Handbook for Excellence in Infant Toddler Programs.* St. Paul, MN: Redleaf Press.

Guldberg, H. (2009) *Reclaiming Childhood: Freedom and Play in an Age of Fear.* London: Routledge.

Hakim, C., Bradley, K., Price, E. and Mitchell, L. (2008) *Little Britons: Financing Childcare Choice.* London: Policy Exchange.

Halliday, M. (1975) *Learning How to Mean.* London: Arnold.

Harms, T., Cryer, D. and Clifford, R.M. (1990) *Infant/Toddler Environment Rating Scale.* New York: Teachers College Press.

High-scope (2014) *Curriculum: The High-Scope Difference: Active Participatory Learning.* Available at: http://www.highscope.org/Content.asp?ContentId=1 (accessed 04/08/2014).

HM Government (2009) *Next Steps for Early Learning and Childcare: Building on the 10 Year Strategy.* London: TSO.

Hoffman, M.L. (1988) Moral development, in M. Bornstein and M. Lamb (eds) *Developmental Psychology: An Advanced Textbook.* Hillsdale, NJ: Erlbaum.

Holmes, J. (1993) *John Bowlby and Attachment Theory.* London: Routledge.

Holmes, J. (2014) *John Bowlby and Attachment Theory.* Hove: Routledge.

Howes, C., Phillips, D.A. and Whitebook, M. (1992) Thresholds of quality: implications for the social development of children in centre-based childcare. *Child Development* 63: 449–60.

I CAN (2004) *Nursery Workers' Poll Says "Turn off the TV".* Available at: www.ican.org.uk/news/news.asp?NewsReference=55 (accessed 08/07/2014).

Jabadao (2011) *Everybody Needs to Play – Rough and Tumble Play.* Available at: http://www.jabadao.org/?p=rough.tumble.play (accessed 12/05/2014).

Jarvis, P. (2009) Building social hardiness for life: rough and tumble play in the early years of primary school, in J. Brock, S. Dodds, P. Jarvis and Y. Olusoga *Perspectives on Play: Learning for Life.* Harlow: Pearson Education.

Karen, R. (1998) *Becoming Attached: First Relationships and How They Shape Our Capacity to Love.* Oxford: Oxford University Press.

Karmiloff-Smith, A. (1992) *Beyond Modularity: A Developmental Perspective on Cognitive Science.* Cambridge, MA: MIT Press.

Karmiloff-Smith, A. (1994) *Baby, It's You.* London: Ebury Press.

Karmiloff-Smith, A. (1995) The extraordinary journey from foetus through infancy. *Journal of Child Psychology and Psychiatry*, 36: 1293–315.

Katz, L. (1988) What should young children be doing? *American Educator*, Summer (28): 44–5.

Katz L. (1993) *Five Perspectives on Quality in Early Childhood Programs* Eric Catalogue No. 208; April 1993.

Katz, L. (1995) *Talks with Teachers of Young Children: A Collection.* Norwood, NJ: Ablex Publishing.

Katz, L., Corlyon, J., La Placa, V. and Hunter, S. (2007) *The Relationship between Parenting and Poverty.* York: The Joseph Rowntree Foundation.

Kellegrew, D. and Youcha, V. (2004) Zero To Three's model of leadership development: knowing and doing in the context of relationships. *Journal of Zero to Three,* 25(2): 6–14.

LaBarre, F. (2001) *On Moving and Being Moved: Nonverbal Behaviour in Clinical Practice.* Hillsdale, NJ: Analytic Press.

Laevers, F. (ed.) (1994) *The Leuven Involvement Scale for Young Children.* Leuven, Belgium: Centre for Experiential Education.

Lally, J.R., Torres, Y.L. and Phelps, P.C. (1997) Caring for infants and toddlers in groups: necessary considerations for emotional, social and cognitive development. *Journal of Zero to Three,* 14(5): 1–8.

Lamont, B. (2009) *Developmental Movement Play.* Available at: http://www.developmentalmovement.org/ (accessed 04/08/2014).

Lawrence, D. (2006) *Enhancing Self-esteem in the Classroom,* 3rd edn. London: Sage.

Leach, P., Sylva, K. and Stein, A. (2006) *The Families, Children and Child Care Study.* Available at: http://www.familieschildrenchildcare.org/fccc_frames_home.html (accessed 29/07/2014).

Ledoux, J. (1998) *The Emotional Brain: The Mysterious Underpinnings of Emotional Life.* New York: Touchstone.

LeVoguer, M. and Pasch, J. (2014) Physical well-being: autonomy and risk taking, in J. Manning-Morton (ed.) *Exploring Well-being in the Early Years.* Maidenhead: Open University Press/McGraw-Hill Education.

Lieberman, A. (1995) *The Emotional Life of the Toddler.* New York: Free Press.

Liverpool City Council Quality Improvement Team (EYFS) (2013–14) Step up for 2-year-olds. Unpublished.

Maccoby, E. (1992) The role of parents in the socialization of children: an historical overview. *Developmental Psychology,* 28: 1006–17.

Manning-Morton, J. (2003) Transitions: supporting children, parents and practitioners to settle into day care. *Early Childhood Practice,* 5(2): 42–52.

Manning-Morton, J. (2004) Birth to three: your guide to developing quality provision. *Nursery World.* 19 August.

Manning-Morton, J. (2006) The personal is professional: professionalism and the birth to threes practitioner. *Contemporary Issues in Early Childhood,* 7(1): 42–52.

Manning-Morton, J. (2011) Not just the tip of the iceberg: psychoanalytic ideas and early years practice, in L. Miller and L. Pound (eds) *Theories and Approaches to Learning in the Early Years.*London: Sage.

Manning-Morton, J. (ed.) (2014) *Exploring Well-being in the Early Years.* Maidenhead: Open University Press/McGraw-Hill Education.

Manning-Morton, J. and Thorp, M. (2003) *Key Times for Play: The First Three Years.* Maidenhead: Open University Press/McGraw-Hill Education.

Manning-Morton, J. and Thorp, M. (2006) *Key Times: Developing High Quality Provision for Children from Birth to Three Years.* Maidenhead: Open University Press/McGraw-Hill Education.

Manning-Morton, J. and Wilson, D. (2011) Addressing emotional well-being for infants, toddlers and young children through the professional development of practitioners. Presentation to the European Early Childhood Education Research Association, August. Unpublished.

Mathers, S., Sylva, K. and Karemaker, J. (2011) *Quality Counts: Evidence from the Evaluation of the Early Education Pilot for Two Year Old Children.* Department of Education and University of Oxford. Available at: http://www.ecersuk.org/resources/ECERS+Network+June+2011+Two+Year+Olds+Oxford.pdf (accessed 24/08/2014).

Matthews, J. (2003) *Drawing and Painting: Children and Visual Representation.* London: Sage.

Maude, P. (2001) *Physical Children, Active Teaching: Investigating Physical Literacy* Buckingham: Open University Press.

Miller, L. (1990) Play as a foundation for learning, in R. Drury, R. Campbell and L. Miller (eds) *Looking at Early Years Education and Care.* London: David Fulton.

Miller, L. (1992) *Understanding Your Baby (Understanding Your Child).* London: Rosendale Press.

Miller, L. (2004) *Understanding Your 2 Year Old.* London: Jessica Kingsley Publishers.

Miller, L. and Pound, L. (2011) *Theories and Approaches to Learning in the Early Years.* London: Sage.

Miller, L., Rustin, M., Rustin, M. and Shuttleworth, J. (eds) (1989) *Closely Observed Infants.* London: Duckworth.

Ministry of Education (1996) *Te Whariki Early Childhood Curriculum.* Wellington, NZ: Learning Media Limited.

Moon, J. (2005) *Reflection in Learning and Professional Development.* Oxford: RoutledgeFalmer.

Morgan, D. (2011) *Rethinking Family Practices.* Basingstoke: Palgrave Macmillan.

Moss, P. and Petrie, P. (2002) *From Children's Services to Children's Spaces.* London: RoutledgeFalmer.

Mukerji, P. and O'Dea, T. (2000) *Understanding Children's Language and Literacy.* London: Stanley Thomas Publishers Ltd.

Munton, T. with Mooney, A., Moss, P., Petrie, P., Clark, A., Woolner, J., Barclay, L., Mallardo, M.R. and Barreau, S. (2002) *Research on Ratios, Group Size and Staff Qualifications and Training in Early Years and Childcare Settings.* London: Thomas Coram Research Unit, Institute of Education, University of London: Queen's Printer.

National Institute of Child Health and Human Development Early Child Care Research Network (2006) Child-care effect sizes for the NICHD Study of Early Child Care and Youth Development. *American Psychologist*, 61(2): 99–116.

National Literacy Trust (2004) *Early Language Advocacy Kit for Early Years Professionals Talk To Your Baby: Developing Language for Life.* Available at: http://www.literacytrust.org.uk/assets/0000/1153/advocacykit.pdf (accessed 23/06/2014).

National Literacy Trust (2014) *Research: The Cognitive Consequences of Early Bilingualism.* Available at: http://www.literacytrust.org.uk/research/nlt_research/2334 (accessed 28/01/2014).

Nutbrown, C. (1999) *Threads of Thinking: Young Children Learning and the Role of Early Education.* London: Paul Chapman Publishing Ltd.

Nutbrown, C. (2012) *Review of Early Education and Childhood Qualifications.* Available at: https://www.gov.uk/government/publications/nutbrown-review-foundations-for-quality (accessed 01/10/14).

Osborne, C. (2004) *Maternal Stress and Mothering Behaviors in Stable and Unstable Families*, Center for Research on Child Well-being: Working Paper # 03-08-FF. Available at: http://crcw.princeton.edu/workingpapers/WP03-08-FF-Osborne.pdf (accessed 01/10/14).

Ouvry, M. (2003) *Exercising Muscles and Minds: Outdoor Play and the Early Years Curriculum.* London: National Children's Bureau.

Owen, S. and Petrie, S. (2006) 'Observe more . . . do less': the approaches of Magda Gerber to parent education, in L. Abbott, and A. Langston (eds) *Parents Matter: Supporting the Birth to Three Framework.* Maidenhead: Open University Press/McGraw-Hill.

Page, J. (2011) Do mothers want professional carers to love their babies? *Journal of Early Childhood Research*, 9(3): 310–23.

Panksepp, J. (1998) *Affective Neuroscience: The Foundations of Human and Animal Emotions.* Oxford: Oxford University Press.

Parten, M. (1932) Social participation among preschool children. *Journal of Abnormal and Social Psychology*, 27: 243–69.

Pasch, J. (2013) Emotion, mastery and meaning – getting connected in the early years. Paper presented at the Expect the Best Conference, June, 2013.

Penn, H. (2008) *Understanding Early Childhood: Issues and Controversies.* Maidenhead: Open University Press/McGraw-Hill.

Petrie, S. and Owen, S. (eds) (2005) *Authentic Relationships in Group Care for Infants and Toddlers, Resources for Infant Educarers (RIE) Principles into Practice.* London: Jessica Kingsley Publishers.

Piaget, J. (1952a) *The Origin of Intelligence in the Child*. London: Routledge and Kegan Paul.

Piaget, J. (1952b) *The Child's Conception of Number*. London: Routledge and Kegan Paul.

Piaget, J. (1959) *The Language and Thought of the Child*. London: Routledge.

Piaget, J. (1962) *Play, Dreams and Imitation in Childhood*. London: Routledge and Kegan Paul.

Piaget, J. and Inhelder, B. (1969) *The Psychology of the Child*. London: Routledge and Kegan Paul.

Piek, J.P. (2006) *Infant Motor Development*. Leeds: Human Kinetics.

Pound, L. (2011) *Influencing Early Childhood Education: Key Figures, Philosophies and Ideas*. Maidenhead: McGraw-Hill.

Pound, L. (2013) *Quick Guides for Early Years: Physical Development*. London: Hodder Education.

Raikes, H. (1993) Relationship duration in infant care: time with a high-ability teacher and infant-teacher attachment. *Early Childhood Research Quarterly*, 8: 309–25.

Rathus, S.A. and Facaro, P. (1988) *Understanding Child Talk Development*. New York: Holt, Rinehart and Winston Inc.

Roberts, R. (2010) *Well-Being from Birth*. London: Sage.

Roberts, Y., Brophy, M. and Bacon, N. (2009) *Parenting and Well Being: Knitting Families Together*. London: The Young Foundation.

Robertson, J. and Robertson, J. (1953) Film: *A Two Year Old Goes to Hospital*. Tavistock Child Development research Unit. Ipswich: Concord Films Council.

Robson, S. (1996) The physical environment, in S. Robson and S. Smedley (eds) *Education in Early Childhood: First Things First*. London: David Fulton.

Robson, S. (2006) *Developing Thinking and Understanding in Young Children*. London: Routledge.

Rothbart, M.K. and Bates, J.E. (1998) Temperament, in W. Damon (series ed.) and N. Eisenberg (vol. ed.), *Handbook of Child Psychology*, Vol. 3: *Social, Emotional and Personality Development*, 5th edn. New York: Wiley.

Rogoff, B. (1990) *Apprenticeship in Thinking: Cognitive Development in Social Context*. Oxford: Oxford University Press.

Rutter, M. (1995) Clinical implications of attachment concepts: retrospect and prospect. *Journal of Child Psychology and Psychiatry*, 36(4): 549–71.

Rutter, M. and Rutter, R. (1993) *Developing Minds: Challenge and Continuity across the Lifespan*. London: Penguin.

Saarni, C. (1984) An observational study of children's attempts to monitor their expressive behavior. *Child Development*, 55: 1504–13.

Sabates, R. and Dex, S. (2012) *Multiple Risk Factors in Young Children's Development*. CLS Working Paper 2012/1. London: IoE Centre for Longitudinal Studies.

Samuel, P. (2012) *Outdoor Learning: Forest School Approach*. Available at: http://www.earlylearninghq.org.uk/earlylearninghq-blog/outdoor-learning-forest-school-approach/ (accessed 22/07/2014).

Schaffer, H.R. (2006) *Key Concepts in Developmental Psychology*. London: Sage.

Schore, A.N. (2001) How parent-infant interactions enhance or inhibit the growth of the developing brain. *Infant Mental Health Journal*, 22: 7–66.

Sharp, P. (2001) *Nurturing Emotional Literacy*. London: Fulton.

Shaw, G.B. (1984) *The Intelligent Woman's Guide to Socialism and Capitalism*. New Brunswick: Transaction Publishers.

Sherborne, V. (1990) *Developmental Movement for Children*. Cambridge: Cambridge University Press.

Sheridan, M., Sharma, A. and Cockerill, H. (2007) *From Birth to Five Years: Children's Developmental Progress*, 3rd edn. London: Routledge.

Shuttleworth, J. (1989) Psychoanalytic theory and infant development, in L. Miller, M. Rustin, M. Rustin and J. Shuttleworth (eds) *Closely Observed Infants*. London: Duckworth.

Siegel, D.J. (1999) *The Developing Mind*. New York: Guilford Press.

Siraj-Blatchford, I. and Clarke, P. (2000) *Supporting Identity, Diversity and Language in the Early Years*. Buckingham: Open University Press.

Slade, A. (1987) A longitudinal study of maternal involvement and symbolic play during the toddler period. *Child Development*, 58: 367–75.

Smith, C. and Vernon, J. (1994) *Day Nurseries at a Crossroads: Meeting the Challenge of Child Care in the Nineties*. London: National Children's Bureau.

Smith, P.K., Cowie, H. and Blades, M. (2011) *Understanding Children's Development*, 5th edn. Chichester: Wiley-Blackwell.

Smith, P.K. and Hart, C.H. (eds) (2011) *The Wiley-Blackwell Handbook of Childhood Social Development*. Malden, MA: Blackwell.

Steiner, C.M. (1974) *Scripts People Live: Transactional Analysis of Life Scripts*. New York: Grove Press.

Stern, D. (1985) *The Interpersonal World of the Infant: A View from Psychoanalysis and Developmental Psychology*. New York: Basic Books.

Stern, D. (1990) *Diary of a Baby*. London: Fontana.

Stern, D. (1998) *The Interpersonal World of the Infant*. London: Karnac Books.

Stern, M. and Karraker, K.H. (1989) Sex stereotyping of infants: a review of gender labelling studies. *Sex Roles*, 20(9/10): 521–2.

Stonehouse, A. (ed.) (1990) *Trusting Toddlers: Programming for One to Three-year-olds in Childcare Centres*. St. Paul, Minnesota: Toys 'n Things Press.

Sylva, K., Melhuish, E., Sammons, P., Siraj-Blatchford, I. and Taggart, B. (2004) *The Effective Provision of Pre-school Education (EPPE) Project: Findings from Pre-school to End of Key Stage 1.* London: Sure Start. Available at: http://www.ioe.ac.uk/RB_Final_Report_3-7.pdf (accessed 12/08/2014).

Taggart, G. (2014) *Compassionate Pedagogy.* Available at: http://prezi.com/ngakqssxikau/compassionate-pedagogy/?utm_campaign=share&utm_medium=copy (accessed 04/08/2014).

Teaching and Learning Scotland (2010) *Pre-Birth to Three: Positive Outcomes for Scotland's Children and Families.* Available at: http://www.educationscotland.gov.uk/Images/PreBirthToThreeBooklet_tcm4-633448.pdf (accessed 13/08/2014).

The Strategy Unit and Department for Education and Skills (2008) *Families in Britain: An Evidence Paper.* London: Cabinet Office.

Thelen, E. and Smith, L.B. (1994) *A Dynamic Systems Approach to the Development of Cognition and Action.* Cambridge, MA: MIT Press.

Thomas, A. and Chess, S. (1980) *The Dynamics of Psychological Development.* New York: Bruner/ Mazel.

Thorp, M. (2003) Observations of play experiences finely tuned for children 0–3. *Early Childhood Practice*, 5(2).

Thorp, M. (2013) Research into the perceptions of a cohort of local authority sponsored practitioners studying a University Certificate in Professional Practice with Children aged Birth to Three focusing on their practice, their sense of themselves as professionals and as learners. Presentation to the European Early Childhood Education Research Association, August. Unpublished.

Tickell, C. (2011) *The Early Years: Foundations for Life, Health and Learning,* London: Department for Education.

Tobin, J. (2004) The disappearance of the body in early years education, in L. Bresler (ed.) *Knowing Bodies, Moving Minds: Towards Embodied Teaching and Learning.* London: Kluwer Academic Publishers.

Tovey, H. (2007) *Playing Outdoors: Spaces and Places, Risks and Challenge.* Maidenhead: McGraw-Hill.

Trevarthen, C. (1998) Explaining emotions in attachment. *Social Development*, 7: 269–72.

Trevarthen, C. (2001) Intrinsic motives for companionship in understanding: their origin, development and significance for infant mental health. *Infant Mental Health Journal*, 22 (1–2): 95–131.

Trevarthen, C. (2002) Learning in companionship. *Education in the North, New Series*, 10: 16–25.

Trevarthen, C. and Aitken, K.J. (1994) Brain development, infant communication and empathy disorders: intrinsic factors in child mental health. *Development and Psychopathology*, 6(4): 597–633.

Trevarthen, C. and Aitken, K.J. (2001) Infant intersubjectivity: research, theory, and clinical applications. *Journal of Child Psychology and Psychiatry*, 42(1): 3–48.

Vincent, C. and Ball, S. (2006) *Childcare, Choice and Class Practices: Middle Class Parents and their Children*. London: Routledge.

Viraj-Babul, N., Rose, A., Moiseeva, N. and Makan, N. (2012) Neural correlates of action understanding in infants: influence of motor experience. *Brain and Behaviour*, 2(3): 237–42.

Vygotsky, L.S. (1966) Play and its role in the mental development of the child, in J. Bruner, A. Jolly and K. Sylva (eds) *Play and its Role in Development and Evolution*. Harmondsworth: Penguin.

Vygotsky, L.S. (1986) *Thought and Language*. Cambridge, MA: The MIT Press.

Waldfogel, J. (2004) Social mobility, life chances, and the early years. *CASE paper 88*. London: Centre for Analysis of Social Exclusion, London School of Economics.

Whalley, M. (2001) Working as a team, in G. Pugh (ed.) *Contemporary Issues in the Early Years*. London: Paul Chapman.

Whalley, M. and the Pen Green Centre Team (2007) *Involving Parents in their Children's Learning*. London: Paul Chapman/Sage Publications.

Whitaker, P. (1995) *Managing to Learn*. London: Cassell.

Whitehead, M.R. (2010) *Language & Literacy in the Early Years 0–7*, 4th edn. London: Sage Publications.

Winnicott, D.W. (1957) *The Child, the Family and the Outside World*. London: Penguin.

Winnicott, D. (1960) The theory of the parent-child relationship. *International Journal of Psychoanalysis*, 41: 585–95.

Winnicott, D.W. (2005) *Playing and Reality*. London: Routledge Classics.

Wolfe, P. and Brandt, R. (1998) What do we know from brain research? *Educational Leadership*, 56(3): 8–13.

Wood, D.J., Bruner, J.S. and Ross, G. (1976) The role of tutoring in problem solving. *Journal of Child Psychiatry and Psychology*, 17(2): 89–100.

Index

The Relationship Worlds of Infants and Toddlers
Multiple Perspectives from Early Years Theory and Practice

Sheila Degotardi and Emma Pearson

ISBN: 978-0-335-26300-4 (Paperback)
eBook: 978-0-335-26301-1
2014

The Relationship Worlds of Infants and Toddlers explores the concept of relationships as a core element of early childhood education and care. Taking as its starting point that children from birth to three learn and develop in a network of relationships, it examines what these relationships look and feel like, how they can be fostered and why they are important for children, educators and families who are involved in early years settings.

Key features include:

- The kinds of relationships that are important in early education and care settings
- Understanding the characteristics and meaning of these relationships
- How to build benefitial relationships in early childhood programmes

www.openup.co.uk

||||| OPEN UNIVERSITY PRESS
McGraw - Hill Education

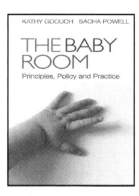

THE BABY ROOM
Principles, Policy and Practice

Kathy Goouch & Sacha Powell

9780335246366 (Paperback)
2013
eBook also available

This book considers babies' development with a view to disseminating good practice in out-of-home daycare for babies and young children. It is informed by a research and development project – the Baby Room Project – which examined the practices, attitudes and qualifications of those working with the youngest children in formal daycare settings.
Drawing on unique snapshots of practice and original research evidence the book considers development issues related to the care of babies and creates a 'Baby Room Charter'.

Key features:

- The book is informed by a research and development project carried out called The Baby Room Project
- Although a staggering 43% of babies are cared for outside of the home in the UK, there has been little or no research undertaken in relation to the care of babies in nurseries until now
- A variety of detailed information from the range of international research on babies' development and care

www.openup.co.uk

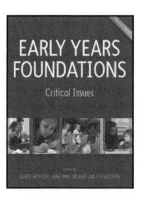

EARLY YEARS FOUNDATIONS
Critical Issues
Second Edition

Janet Moyles, Jane Payler &
Jan Georgeson (Eds)

9780335262649 (Paperback)
February 2014

eBook also available

Among the many challenges facing early years professionals, there
are continual dilemmas arising between perceptions of good
practice, the practicalities of provision and meeting OfSTED
requirements. This exciting and innovative new edition supports
practitioners in thinking through their responsibilities in tackling
some of the many challenges they encounter, for example, that
children are still perceived as 'deficit' in some way and in need of
'being school ready' rather than as developing individuals who have
a right to a childhood and appropriate early education.

Key features:

- Pedagogy
- Working with parents
- Difference and diversity

www.openup.co.uk

OPEN UNIVERSITY PRESS
McGraw - Hill Education

Printed in Germany
by Amazon Distribution
GmbH, Leipzig